How Should the World Respond to Global Warming?

Stuart A. Kallen

INCONTROVERSY

ReferencePoint
Press®

San Diego, CA

© 2010 ReferencePoint Press, Inc.

For more information, contact:
ReferencePoint Press, Inc.
PO Box 27779
San Diego, CA 92198
www.ReferencePointPress.com

Picture credits:
AP Images: 7, 12, 20, 21, 26, 29, 32, 34, 40, 51, 52, 57, 63, 65, 70, 73, 79, 80
Istockphoto.com: 9
Landov: 42, 47, 66
Science Photo Library: 13, 15

LIBRARY OF CONGRESS CATALOGING-IN-PUBLICATION DATA

Kallen, Stuart A., 1955–
  How should the world respond to global warming? / by Stuart A. Kallen.
    p. cm. — (In controversy series)
  Includes bibliographical references and index.
  ISBN-13: 978-1-60152-086-9 (hardback)
  ISBN-10: 1-60152-086-7 (hardback)
  1. Global warming—Juvenile literature. 2. Global warming—Prevention—Juvenile literature.
I. Title.
  QC981.8.G56K35 2009
  363.738'74—dc22
                                                            2009002282

Contents

Foreword

In 2008, as the U.S. economy and economies worldwide were falling into one of the worst recessions in modern history, most Americans had difficulty comprehending the complexity, magnitude, and scope of what was happening. As is often the case with a complex, controversial issue such as this historic global economic recession, looking at the problem as a whole can be overwhelming and often does not lead to understanding. One way to better comprehend such a large issue or event is to break it into smaller parts. The intricacies of global economic recession may be difficult to understand, but one can gain insight by instead beginning with an individual contributing factor such as the real estate market. When examined through a narrower lens, complex issues become clearer and easier to evaluate.

This is the idea behind ReferencePoint Press's *In Controversy* series. The series examines the complex, controversial issues of the day by breaking them into smaller pieces. Rather than looking at the stem cell research debate as a whole, a title would examine an important aspect of the debate such as *Is Stem Cell Research Necessary?* or *Is Embryonic Stem Cell Research Ethical?* By studying the central issues of the debate individually, researchers gain a more solid and focused understanding of the topic as a whole.

Each book in the series provides a clear, insightful discussion of the issues, integrating facts and a variety of contrasting opinions for a solid, balanced perspective. Personal accounts and direct quotes from academic and professional experts, advocacy groups, politicians, and others enhance the narrative. Sidebars add depth to the discussion by expanding on important ideas and events. For quick reference, a list of key facts concludes every chapter. Source notes, an annotated organizations list, bibliography, and index provide student researchers with additional tools for papers and class discussion.

The *In Controversy* series also challenges students to think critically about issues, to improve their problem-solving skills, and to sharpen their ability to form educated opinions. As President Barack Obama stated in a March 2009 speech, success in the twenty-first century will not be measurable merely by students' ability to "fill in a bubble on a test but whether they possess 21st century skills like problem-solving and critical thinking and entrepreneurship and creativity." Those who possess these skills will have a strong foundation for whatever lies ahead.

No one can know for certain what sort of world awaits today's students. What we can assume, however, is that those who are inquisitive about a wide range of issues; open-minded to divergent views; aware of bias and opinion; and able to reason, reflect, and reconsider will be best prepared for the future. As the international development organization Oxfam notes, "Today's young people will grow up to be the citizens of the future: but what that future holds for them is uncertain. We can be quite confident, however, that they will be faced with decisions about a wide range of issues on which people have differing, contradictory views. If they are to develop as global citizens all young people should have the opportunity to engage with these controversial issues."

In Controversy helps today's students better prepare for tomorrow. An understanding of the complex issues that drive our world and the ability to think critically about them are essential components of contributing, competing, and succeeding in the twenty-first century.

A Scientific and Political Problem

In January 2007 the National Climatic Data Center (NCDC) announced that the previous year had been the warmest ever recorded in the United States. The year was marked by severe droughts throughout the southern, western, and plains states. In some areas the period between October 2005 and June 2006 was the driest in 111 years of record keeping. The droughts intensified wildfires that swept across the West, making 2006 the worst fire season ever, with 9.8 million acres burned. Meanwhile, in the Northeast and mid-Atlantic states, numerous records were set for heavy rainfall and flooding. Summer heat waves had a devastating effect in big cities from New York City to Los Angeles, where 225 people died from heat-related problems. When asked to explain the reasons for the deadly weather, Jay Lawrimore, monitoring chief for the NCDC stated: "There's no denying that climate change is occurring, and warmer winters and warmer years are more common for that reason. What we're seeing is just becoming so much more common."[1]

Lawrimore also noted that in 2006 the annual average temperature was 55°F (2.8°C), or 2.2°F (1.2°C) above average. And the following year turned out to be the second warmest year in history, with its own share of weather-related disasters. Looking back on weather data from years past, the NCDC determined that 8 of the 10 hottest years on record occurred since 1995.

Climate change, also known as global warming, is defined as the increase in the average temperature of Earth's air and the oceans. These average temperatures have been rising since 1955 and are expected to increase well into the future. The United Nations Intergovernmental Panel on Climate Change (IPCC) claims a 95 percent certainty that the temperature increases are directly caused by human activities that produce carbon dioxide, methane, and nitrous oxide. These gases are creating an imbalance in the greenhouse effect, a natural part of Earth's climate cycle.

French mathematician Jean Baptiste Joseph Fourier was the first to describe the greenhouse effect in 1824. Fourier noted that Earth's atmosphere—made up of water and tiny amounts of carbon dioxide, methane gas, and other components—acts like the glass in a greenhouse. The atmosphere allows solar radiation, or sunlight, to warm Earth, and it also prevents about 30 percent of that radiation from leaving Earth. This keeps the planet warm enough for human habitation. Without the greenhouse effect, the average temperature on Earth would hover around 0°F (-17.8°C).

A firefighter tries to slow the advance of a massive fire fueled by hot, dry winds in Southern California in 2006. Some scientists say global warming is to blame for high heat and drought in the West and extreme weather in other parts of the country.

Greenhouse Gases

Industrial activity is responsible for increasing the greenhouse gases in the atmosphere, and most scientists believe that this has led to a warmer planet. Carbon dioxide, known by its chemical formula CO_2, has gained the most attention as a global warming gas because it makes up about 70 percent of greenhouse gases. Carbon dioxide is generated when fossil fuels (coal, oil, and natural gas) are burned to produce electricity, power factories, heat houses, and fuel automobiles. Carbon dioxide is also created when forests are cut down or burned.

Scientists have been able to measure the historic amounts of CO_2 in the atmosphere by analyzing tiny air bubbles trapped in Arctic ice. In 2008 atmospheric carbon dioxide concentrations were higher than at any time in the past 650,000 years. And as energy consumption continues to grow in the coming years, the IPCC predicts that CO_2 emissions will increase anywhere from 35 to 450 percent by 2100. This will cause the atmosphere to warm by 2° to 11.5°F (1.1° to 6.3°C).

If the IPCC predictions are true, life on Earth will change radically in the coming century. Scientists believe that rising global temperatures will cause sea levels to rise, polar ice caps to melt, and extreme weather events such as droughts, floods, wildfires, and hurricanes to increase. People will also be affected by changes in agricultural production, species extinction, an increase in disease, and threats to economic security.

Politics and Science

The alarming predictions by the IPCC have motivated many nations to implement plans to reduce global warming gas emissions. However, fossil fuels are central to the world economy. Changing the way society performs basic tasks such as traveling, heating and lighting homes, and growing food has proved to be difficult.

Japan, the world's fifth largest producer of CO_2, is a good example of a country that has run into resistance when trying to reduce emissions. Since 2004 the Ministry of Environment has made four proposals that would levy a tax on the burning of fossil fuels. This money would be used to institute anti–global warming

measures such as planting forests and conducting research into clean energy systems.

The proposed tax was small, about $21 a ton. It would add only 4.3 cents to the price of a gallon of gas. And Japanese industry would pay about 5 cents for every 2.2 pounds of coal burned. The tax proposal would have cost individual consumers about $210 a year. But Japan's auto, steel, and electricity producers together would have jointly paid about $380 million, and they strongly opposed the measure. Industry leaders stated that the tax would hinder Japan's economy and reduce its ability to compete against the growing economies of China and India. Meanwhile, Japanese environmentalists complained that the tax was so small that it would not force industry and consumers to reduce fossil fuel consumption. By 2007 the idea of a carbon tax, as it is called, was dropped. The next year Japanese CO_2 production rose to record levels even as government officials pledged to reduce emissions by 6 percent.

Researchers predict that climate change could negatively affect Japanese rice, wheat, and fruit production; and rising sea levels might permanently flood parts of the island nation. But Japanese citizens are reluctant to pay more for their energy consumption.

Bare ground stretches for miles where trees have been cleared for industry in Brazil's Amazon rain forest. The loss of trees leads to higher levels of carbon dioxide, which contributes to global warming.

The environmental struggles in Japan are mirrored in the United States, Eastern Europe, China, India, and elsewhere. In April 2009 the U.S. Environmental Protection Agency (EPA) formally declared CO_2 and five other heat-trapping gases to be pollutants that endanger public health. With this declaration, the United States for the first time begins a process that will lead to regulation of these gases. The EPA declaration and the process of adopting new regulations mark a continuation of the political debate over how to respond to global warming. Supporters say new regulations will bring long-term social and economic benefits while opponents warn that such regulations will raise energy costs and lead to job losses.

With powerful interests on both sides holding such different views, the fight against global warming is not only a scientific but a political problem as well. While many worry about the damage from global warming, it has been difficult for governments to implement solutions without harming their economic interests.

FACTS

- In April 2009 the EPA formally declared that six heat-trapping gases pose a risk to public health. The six gases are carbon dioxide, methane, nitrous oxide, hydrofluorocarbons, perfluorocarbons, and sulfur hexafluoride.

- Average temperatures have climbed 1.4°F (0.7°C) around the world in recent decades.

- The years between 1988 and 2008 were warmer than any in the previous 400 years of weather record keeping.

What Are the Origins of the Global Warming Issue?

In January 1998 scientist Wallace S. Broecker told the *New York Times*, "The climate system is an angry beast and we are poking it with sticks."[2] Broecker, of Columbia University's Lamont-Doherty Earth Observatory, was commenting on the growing evidence during the late 1990s that the climate was changing dramatically and human behavior was inviting disaster.

Broecker is a geochemist, oceanographer, and paleoclimatologist, or one who studies historic climate patterns. In 1975 he published a research paper in the journal *Science* called "Climate Change: Are We on the Brink of a Pronounced Global Warming?" This was one of the earliest media references to climate change and global warming. However, a few scientists had been aware of the problem for several decades.

Carbon Sinks

In the 1950s oceanographer Roger Revelle began studying the way Earth's oceans were interacting with carbon dioxide, or CO_2. Carbon dioxide is a gas produced by volcanic eruptions. It is also exhaled by land animals during the breathing process. Revelle was not interested in these naturally produced forms of CO_2 but in the levels of carbon dioxide added to the atmosphere by humans burning fossil fuels.

11

Working out of the Scripps Institution of Oceanography in La Jolla, California, Revelle understood that oceans are nature's carbon sinks. This means that the CO_2 in the atmosphere sinks into seawater, which contains billions of tiny phytoplankton. These microscopic creatures absorb the CO_2, then fall to the bottom of the sea when they die, trapping carbon in layers of sediment on the ocean floor. Until the 1950s scientists believed that the oceans would trap manmade, or anthropogenic, CO_2 forever without any problems. But in 1957 Revelle discovered that the oceans were absorbing CO_2 at much slower rates than previously expected. He described his observations in a paper he coauthored with chemist Hans Suess, concluding that the oceans would eventually reach a saturation point where they could no longer absorb the CO_2. This would enhance the greenhouse effect and cause Earth to warm over time.

Roger Revelle, pictured here in 1957, discovered that the world's oceans were absorbing carbon dioxide more slowly than was previously understood. He concluded that this process might eventually stop altogether, causing the Earth to warm.

The Keeling Curve

Revelle's findings were of particular interest to scientist Charles David Keeling, who invented a device called a manometer for measuring carbon dioxide in the atmosphere. This machine measures CO_2 in parts per million (ppm) and showed that in 1957 the atmosphere contained 315 ppm of carbon dioxide. As other scientists would later discover, this number was higher than the historical average. Before people began burning large amounts of coal during the industrial revolution in the late 1700s, CO_2 concentrations in the atmosphere held steady at 280 ppm for tens of thousands of years.

In order to obtain extremely accurate CO_2 readings, Keeling set up his manometer at the Mauna Loa Observatory in Hawaii. At this site, 10,000 feet (3,048m) above sea level, the readings would not be tainted by air pollution from cars, cities, and factories. Keeling collected CO_2 data at this remote location year after year and entered the readings on a chart. By the mid-1960s he was alarmed to discover that atmospheric CO_2 levels were continually increasing. His chart showed a steady upward trend, which is now called the Keeling Curve.

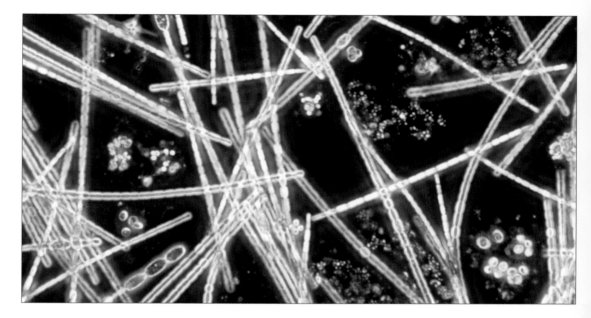

Despite his discovery, few people outside of scientific circles understood the importance of Keeling's work. He struggled tirelessly to obtain funding for his obscure research project conducted from a remote mountaintop in the middle of the Pacific Ocean. Commenting on the significance of Keeling's efforts, British climate researcher Andrew Manning states: "Without this curve, and Professor Keeling's tireless work, there is no question that our understanding and acceptance of human-induced global warming would be 10–20 years less advanced than it is today."[3]

Phytoplankton, minute free-floating aquatic organisms, absorb and trap carbon dioxide on the ocean floor. This process helps to control greenhouse gases.

"Surprised and Disturbed"

In 1968 Revelle became a professor of natural sciences at Harvard and began using the Keeling Curve as a teaching tool in his classroom. One of Revelle's students was future vice president and environmental activist Al Gore, who said Revelle "was surprised and disturbed by how quickly CO_2 was building up. . . . He knew that this path our civilization had taken would send us careening toward catastrophe, unless the trend could be reversed."[4]

Gore was elected to Congress in 1976 where he soon organized the first congressional hearing on global warming. Revelle was called as the leadoff witness. Gore assumed that when Revelle explained the CO_2 problem to other members of Congress, they would be equally alarmed. He found, however, that his colleagues were either uninterested or did not believe that rising carbon dioxide levels presented a problem.

Gore says he encountered similar apathy and resistance when he became a senator in 1984. However, by that time CO_2 levels at Mauna Loa were rising dramatically, and some of the country's leading scientists were taking notice. At NASA's Goddard Institute for Space Studies (GISS) in New York, director James Hansen developed computer models based on the Mauna Loa data. In 1986 Hansen created a stir when he told a congressional committee that "the global warming predicted in the next 20 years will make the Earth warmer than it has been in the past 100,000 years."[5]

At the time of Hansen's testimony, only about half of all Americans had ever heard of global warming, and most thought it was a problem for future generations. However, in June 1988 severe heat waves and a major drought struck the central United States. This attracted the attention of the media as reporters began to speculate on the sudden change in climate. Around the same time, Colorado senator Timothy Wirth, chairman of the United States Senate Committee on Energy and Natural Resources, held a meeting about global warming. He called Hansen to testify on June 23, a day when the temperature in Washington, D.C., hit a record high. Hansen later described what he told the committee:

> [The] world was getting warmer on [decade-to-decade] time scales, which I said could be stated with 99 percent confidence. . . . [In] our climate model there was a tendency for an increase in the frequency and the severity of heat waves and droughts with global warming. . . . [And] it's time to stop waffling so much and say that the greenhouse effect is here and affecting our climate now.[6]

Global Warming Controversy

Climate scientists caution that the weather patterns from a single year should not be equated with long-term global warming pat-

> "The climate system is an angry beast and we are poking it with sticks."[2]
>
> — Wallace S. Broecker, scientist at Lamont-Doherty Earth Observatory.

CARBON DIOXIDE AT MAUNA LOA OBSERVATORY, HAWAII

1958-1974 SCRIPPS
1974-1990 NOAA

terns. But the record-breaking weather of the summer of 1988 became closely associated with global warming in the pubic arena. By the end of the year, 58 percent of Americans said they had heard of or read about global warming, a 20 percent jump since 1981. The issue also gained more attention within government circles. As environmental advocate Michael Oppenheimer told the *New York Times*, "I've never seen an environmental issue mature so quickly, shifting from science to the policy realm almost overnight."[7]

The public attention to global warming gave environmental groups a new focus. Within a short period, Greenpeace, the Environmental Defense Fund, and the Sierra Club made reducing carbon dioxide their main concern. But environmental groups took up the cause of global warming during an era of strong backlash against the so-called green, or environmental, movement. When Ronald Reagan was elected president in 1980, he often criticized government for placing too many environmental regulations on businesses. As Thomas Friedman explains in *Hot, Flat, and Crowded*: "Reagan ran not only against government in general but

A climate scientist displays a Keeling Curve graph, showing rising levels of carbon dioxide in the atmosphere at Hawaii's Mauna Loa volcano between the 1950s and 1980s. The Keeling Curve is named for scientist Charles David Keeling, the inventor of a device that measures carbon dioxide in the atmosphere.

against environmental regulation in particular. He . . . turned environmental regulation into a much more partisan and polarizing issue than it had ever been before. It has been so ever since.[8]

Members of the Reagan administration laid out a plan to resist CO_2 regulations. They believed that the best way to deal with global warming concerns was "to raise the many uncertainties"[9] of global warming.

It was not just the Reagan administration that opposed new environmental regulations. The major emitters of global warming emissions included politically powerful industries such as oil companies, coal producers, steelmakers, and automobile manufacturers. These industries employed millions of people across the country and were concerned that global warming regulations would raise the cost of doing business. This would not only threaten profits but force companies to lay off workers, creating widespread unemployment.

With the Reagan administration leading the way, big business put together an organized plan to resist environmental regulations. Scientists working for large corporations conducted industry-financed studies that denied temperatures were rising or else blamed global warming on sunspots or long-term weather patterns that had nothing to do with human activity. As the scientists published elaborate studies, oil companies and others ran ads in popular magazines assuring the public that global warming was not a problem.

In order to further promote their viewpoints in Congress, the courts, and the media, wealthy conservatives and major corporations joined together to form policy institutes, or think tanks. The Competitive Enterprise Institute (CEI), founded in 1984, became one of the leading policy institutes dedicated to changing public attitudes against global warming. The institute was funded with millions of dollars donated by ExxonMobil, the American Petroleum Institute, Dow Chemical, and General Motors. It publicized the theme that climate change would create a "milder, greener, more prosperous world."[10]

The CEI was among several dozen pro-business policy institutes formed in the 1980s to oppose the goals of environmental

"It's time to stop waffling so much and say that the greenhouse effect is here and affecting our climate now."[6]

— James Hansen, director, Goddard Institute for Space Studies.

Climate Change or Global Warming?

The terms *global warming* and *climate change* are both used when discussing problems caused by rising levels of carbon dioxide and other gases. However, climate change is becoming more common. Global warming describes the rising surface temperatures caused by the increase in manmade carbon dioxide, nitrous oxide, and other gases in the atmosphere. Global climate change, on the other hand, describes the environmental effects of global warming. Climate change problems include rising sea levels, increasingly severe storms, droughts, and so on. Climate change might result in record-setting snowstorms in one part of the globe and brutal heat waves in another region. Despite the technical differences most media sources use the terms climate change and global warming interchangeably.

groups. By the late 1980s members of these groups were questioning global warming science in editorial columns and on television news programs and radio talks shows. With this new input, the media began to cover climate change differently. As one unnamed historian stated, the new debate was "transforming the issue from one of scientific concern to one of political controversy."[11]

By the 1990s American environmental groups and industries that relied on fossil fuels were engaged in a sustained public relations effort to sway people to their respective sides. This created a sense of ambivalence among the public. A 1995 ABC poll showed that while 80 percent believed global warming was happening, only 41 percent believed it was an extremely important issue in their lives.

Climate Change Summits

While Americans remained divided on the importance of global warming, international concern continued to grow. In 1988 the United Nations (UN) and the World Meteorological Organization (WMO) established the Intergovernmental Panel on Climate

Change (IPCC) to study climate change. The panel, which remains active today, is composed of 2,500 experts from more than 60 countries who work in widely divergent fields such as climatology, ecology, economics, medicine, and oceanography. Because of this wide range of expertise, the IPCC has been viewed by scientists and environmentalists as the most credible organization studying global warming. The IPCC released its first climate change reports in 1990, which states: "We are certain emissions resulting from human activities are substantially increasing the atmospheric concentrations of the greenhouse gases: carbon dioxide, methane . . . and nitrous oxide. These increases will enhance the greenhouse effect, resulting on average in an additional warming of the Earth's surface."[12]

After the IPCC released a report with similar conclusions in January 1992, the United Nations Convention on Climate Change was formed to address the issue. On June 2 in Rio de Janeiro the group held a 12-day conference known as the Earth Summit. The summit was attended by heads of state from 102 countries. About 17,000 others from environmental groups and nongovernmental organizations (NGOs) also attended the summit.

Delegates at the Earth Summit produced the Framework Convention on Climate Change (FCCC), a treaty that was signed within months by government leaders in 154 countries. The FCCC stated that industrial nations should take immediate steps to reduce global warming emissions. However, the framework was completely voluntary. Signatories did not have to set specific goals for reduction, no time frame was set for reducing emissions, and no penalties were proposed for those who violated the recommendations.

In 1997, five years after the Earth Summit, signatories of the FCCC met again in Kyoto, Japan. By this time it was obvious to most attendees that global warming was increasing. The FCCC decided that member nations should set targets to reduce their CO_2 emissions. They also created a system to reduce greenhouse gases. This system, called cap and trade, provides financial incentives to polluters to lower their carbon dioxide emissions.

"We are certain emissions resulting from human activities are substantially increasing the atmospheric concentrations of the greenhouse gases: carbon dioxide, methane . . . and nitrous oxide."[12]

— Intergovernmental Panel on Climate Change, a climate change research institution of the United Nations.

Cap and trade authorizes governments or an international body to set a limit, or cap, on the amount of global warming pollution an industry can emit. Companies are issued emission permits allowing them to produce a specific amount of global warming gas every year. Companies that pollute less can sell their credits on the market to those who pollute more. This transfer of permits is referred to as a trade. In this way, the buyer is paying a charge for polluting, while the seller is being rewarded for having reduced emissions.

United States Rejects Kyoto Protocol

The cap-and-trade system, along with proposed reductions in global warming gases, was written into a treaty called the Kyoto Protocol. In the United States, President Bill Clinton wanted to sign the protocol, but the treaty had to be approved by Congress. According to physicist Spencer Wert, the Kyoto Protocol created a major political controversy:

> Pressure on Congress [to reject the treaty] came mainly from anti-government conservatives and industries that depended on fossil fuels. Right-leaning think tanks re-doubled their efforts to deny that global warming posed a threat. . . . A typical argument in the pamphlets, op-ed essays, and press conferences was to point with horror at the specter of a tax on emissions. They claimed it would impose a dreadful rise in gasoline prices, supposedly intol-erable to Americans. . . . The opponents also appealed to nationalism by warning that other countries would seize an economic advantage over the United States unless all reduced their emissions together.[13]

Because of the strong resistance, Clinton never submitted the treaty for congressional approval. This left the United States as the only developed nation besides Australia that refused to implement the Kyoto Protocol.

Hurricane Katrina

In 2001 George W. Bush, a former Texas oilman, was sworn in as president of the United States. Bush did not support the Kyoto

Flood waters submerge houses, streets, and cars in a New Orleans neighborhood after Hurricane Katrina hit the Gulf Coast in 2005. That year saw a record number of hurricanes, which some experts have linked to global warming.

Protocol and his administration was hostile to any new environmental regulations. And after the terrorist attacks of September 11, 2001, and the invasion of Iraq in 2003, the issue of global warming was barely mentioned in the media or halls of Congress.

On August 29, 2005, climate made the front pages once again when Hurricane Katrina slammed into the Gulf Coast. As a powerful category 3 hurricane, Katrina caused major damage from Florida to Texas. But the hurricane's effects were most catastrophic in New Orleans where 140-mile-per-hour winds (225 kmph) and a storm surge caused major damage. The levees that protected New Orleans failed, and 80 percent of the city flooded. At least 1,836 people were killed, and the storm caused a record $81 billion in damages.

Three weeks after Katrina struck, Hurricane Rita, a category 5 storm, hit the same region. A few weeks later, Hurricane Wilma—the most powerful hurricane ever measured—devastated parts of Mexico and Florida. In total, the region experienced a record 27 hurricanes in the region in 2005, and experts believe that the increase was related to global warming.

An Inconvenient Truth

In 2006, while many New Orleans neighborhoods remained in ruins, Al Gore released the film *An Inconvenient Truth*. The movie discussed the work of Revelle, Keeling, and others and shone a new spotlight on global warming. Filled with imagery from dozens of countries that showed deforestation, floods, droughts, retreating glaciers, and melting ice caps, the film provided stunning visual examples of an overheated atmosphere. Gore also used charts and graphs to demonstrate rising CO_2 levels and temperatures.

An Inconvenient Truth was an extremely popular film and became the fourth-highest-grossing documentary in history. And

Former vice president Al Gore (left) and director Davis Guggenheim accept the Oscar in 2007 after their film, An Inconvenient Truth, *won an Academy Award for Best Documentary. The film brought to light the issue of climate change.*

"The Future Is Knocking"

In 2007 former vice president Al Gore won a Nobel Peace Prize for his efforts in alerting the world to the dangers of global warming. An excerpt of his December 10, 2007, acceptance speech appears below.

[Today] we dumped another 70 million tons of global warming pollution into the thin shell of atmosphere surrounding our planet, as if it were an open sewer. . . . As a result, the Earth has a fever, and the fever is rising. The experts have told us it is not a passing affliction that will heal by itself. . . .

As temperature extremes have increased, tens of thousands have lost their lives. We are recklessly burning and clearing our forest and driving more and more species into extinction; the very web of life on which we depend is being ripped and frayed. . . .

The future is knocking at our door right now. Make no mistake: The next generation will ask us one of two questions. Either they will ask "What were you thinking? Why didn't you act?" or they will ask instead, "How did you find the moral courage to rise and successfully resolve a crisis that so many said was impossible to solve?

Al Gore, "Nobel Lecture," Nobel Foundation, December 10, 2007. http://nobelprize.org.

the movie, which won an Academy Award for Best Documentary Feature, provided one of the clearest learning tools ever created for bringing the issue of global warming to a wide audience.

With public awareness of global warming at record levels, the January 2007 report by the IPCC received wide coverage in the media. The report claims a 95 percent certainty that the global mean temperature increase can be directly traced to human activities that release greenhouse gases into the atmosphere. The report warns of more frequent warm spells, heat waves, and heavy rainfall. It also warns of an increase in droughts, tropical cyclones, and extreme high tides.

In October 2007 Al Gore and the IPCC jointly shared the Nobel Peace Prize. According to the Nobel Committee, Gore and the IPCC were given the award "for their efforts to build up and disseminate greater knowledge about man-made climate change, and to lay the foundations for the measures that are needed to counteract such change."[14]

The Defining Moment

By 2008 an ABC poll showed that more than 80 percent of all Americans understood that Earth was warming, and an equal number said it was an important issue to them personally. Over 70 percent of those polled said they had cut back on their energy use to make a smaller carbon footprint—that is, to produce less greenhouse gases.

Although awareness about global warming is now evident among the public and policy makers, the problem continues to grow. In May 2008 the National Oceanic and Atmospheric Administration (NOAA) announced that CO_2 levels were at a record high. Carbon dioxide had increased to 387 ppm, up almost 40 percent since the industrial revolution began and the highest level for at least the last 650,000 years. And experts predicted a 10 percent rise in greenhouse gas emissions by 2010 rather than the 5.2 percent reduction called for in the Kyoto Protocol.

While the Kyoto goals are not being met, the treaty has forced governments, industry, and the general public to take the first steps necessary to confront the problem, which is expected to increase in severity. As IPCC chairman Rajendra Pachauri told reporters when issuing the 2007 report, "If there's no action before 2012, that's too late. What we do in the next two or three years will determine our future. This is the defining moment."[15]

"If there's no action before 2012, that's too late. What we do in the next two or three years will determine our future."[15]

— Rajendra Pachauri, chairman of the IPCC.

FACTS

- Hurricanes in both the Atlantic and the Pacific have increased in duration and intensity by about 50 percent since 1970.

- In 2005 more than 200 cities in the western United States broke all-time records for high temperatures.

- A cap-and-trade tax of $100 a ton in the United States would raise gasoline prices by about $1 a gallon.

- Al Gore dedicated 100 percent of the profits from the movie *An Inconvenient Truth* to a global warming educational campaign.

- President George W. Bush did not support the Kyoto Protocol partly because the treaty exempted China, one of the world's largest producers of carbon dioxide.

How Should Developing Nations Respond?

In the late 1700s coal-fired steam engines began performing work that had been done for thousands of years by animal power, water power, and human muscle. These engines powered the industrial revolution that completely changed the economic foundations of Great Britain, France, Germany, the United States, and other Western nations. Through the consumption of coal, oil, gasoline, kerosene, and natural gas, millions of people were enriched beyond the dreams of previous generations.

The wealth generated by the massive consumption of fossil fuels in what is called the developed world only affected a small percentage of people on the planet. As of 2009 around 800 million people lived in industrial or developed nations that included the United States, Canada, Japan, and countries in western Europe. The other 6 billion people on Earth live in nonindustrial, or developing nations. Nearly half of those people live in just 2 countries, China and India. And the economies of these 2 countries, based on energy-intensive manufacturing, have grown at an unprecedented rate since the 1990s.

China's economy alone has expanded at a remarkable pace of 11 percent a year for the past decade. As a result, tens of millions of Chinese people are now living a lifestyle that is similar in many ways to the American lifestyle. They are buying new cars, eating American-style fast food, and moving into single-family homes stocked with computers, modern appliances, wide-screen televisions, iPods, and cell phones. This is good news for citizens of a nation traditionally associated with dire poverty. However, as a result of their growing coal- and oil-dependent economies, China and India are now major producers of global warming emissions. And the numbers tell the story.

In 1990 China and India together accounted for 13 percent of world carbon dioxide emissions; in 2008 their combined share had risen to 25 percent. And experts predict that by 2030, carbon dioxide emissions from China and India combined will account for 34 percent of total world emissions, with China alone responsible for 28 percent.

China is only one of dozens of developing countries where millions of people can now afford to live like middle-class Americans. Similar situations are found in Vietnam, Thailand, Indonesia, Malaysia, Brazil, Russia, and eastern Europe. New factories,

Cars drive on a highway in Beijing, China, shrouded in fog and heavily polluted air. China's growing dependence on coal and oil have propelled it into the position of being a major producer of greenhouse gases.

skyscrapers, and gleaming shopping malls, all dependent on electricity produced with cheap fossil fuels, are springing up in the Middle East, Southeast Asia, South America, and elsewhere.

People who are enjoying prosperity for the first time are largely uninterested in reducing CO_2 emissions. They point out that Americans have enjoyed the comforts of an industrialized society for generations, and now it is their turn. As an unnamed Egyptian cabinet minister told Thomas Friedman, "It is like the developed world ate all the hors d'oeuvres, all the entrees, and all the desserts and then invited the developing world for a little coffee and asked us to split the whole bill."[16]

The Risk of Hunger

It is understandable that people in developing nations want their economies to grow rapidly. However, these countries have fewer resources and less technology than developed nations. Therefore, it will be difficult for them to deal with global warming problems such as rising sea levels, increasingly severe heat waves, and tropical storms.

According to a 2007 report by the United Nations Food and Agriculture Organization, global warming could lead to widespread starvation in developing nations. According to Jacques Diouf, the director general of the organization, "a rise in global temperatures would increase food production in most industrialized countries, which mostly have colder climates. [However, in nations closer to the equator] . . . crop yield potential is likely to decline for even small global temperature rises, which would increase the risk of hunger."[17] India alone could lose 18 percent of its annual rice crop production.

Climate change is already threatening water supplies in India and China. In 2005 researchers discovered that the glaciers in the Himalaya Mountains were melting at an alarming rate. These glaciers store the largest supply of freshwater outside the polar ice caps.

Himalayan waters feed seven great Asian rivers including the Ganges in India, the Yangtze in China, the Indus in Pakistan, and the Mekong in Southeast Asia. Ancient civilizations grew and

"[Our] people have a right to economic and social development and to discard the ignominy of widespread poverty."[18]

—Manmohan Singh, prime minister of India.

India's Vision of Sustainable Development

India's prime minister Manmohan Singh signed the nation's first National Action Plan on Climate Change (NAPCC) in June 2008. An excerpt of the speech he gave on this occasion appears below.

India has a . . . legacy which treats Nature as a source of nurture and not as a dark force to be conquered and harnessed to human endeavor. There is a high value placed in our culture to the concept of living in harmony with Nature, recognizing the delicate threads of common destiny that hold our universe together. The time has come for us to draw deep from this tradition and launch India and its billion people on a path of ecologically sustainable development. . . . [I] believe that ecologically sustainable development need not be in contradiction to achieving our growth objectives. . . . Our people want higher standards of living, but they also want clean water to drink, fresh air to breathe and a green earth to walk on. The National Action Plan . . . incorporates India's vision of sustainable development and the steps we must take to implement it.

Manmohan Singh, "Prime Minister's Speech on Release of Climate Change Action Plan," Prime Minister of India, June 30, 2008. www.pmindia.nic.in.

thrived along the shores of these rivers, and today one-sixth of the world's population depends on their waters for survival.

As the glaciers melt, researchers expect major flooding in cities thousands of miles from the Himalayan Mountains. But as the glaciers shrink, water levels will decline, causing major problems for people in China, India, and elsewhere by the middle of the twenty-first century.

India's National Mission

In reaction to the dire predictions, India's prime minister Manmohan Singh signed the nation's first National Action Plan on Climate Change (NAPCC) in June 2008. The plan outlines current and future policies and programs meant to mitigate the effects of global warming.

The NAPCC focuses on reforestation because trees and other plants help reduce global warming by consuming CO_2 and producing oxygen during photosynthesis. To deal with the Himalaya water issue, the government instituted the National Mission for Sustaining the Himalayan Ecosystem. This plan will reduce logging and development in the Himalayan forests. The National Mission for a Green India was instituted to plant trees on about 90 million acres of deforested land. When completed, this program will increase the nation's forest cover from 23 percent to 33 percent of its total territory.

Since coal-fired power plants create so much of India's CO_2 pollution, the National Solar Mission was instituted to promote the development and use of solar energy for power generation. Although solar power is more expensive than coal, planners are hoping that increased production of photovoltaic (PV) solar cells will

Melting water from glaciers high in the Himalayas (pictured) feeds many of Asia's major rivers and lakes. Millions of people depend on these rivers and lakes for their water, but scientists warn that global warming is causing the glaciers to melt too quickly.

lower costs. India is also emphasizing energy efficiency, which is the cheapest way to reduce carbon dioxide emissions. The NAPCC contains a plan called the National Mission for Enhanced Energy Efficiency to promote energy conservation.

A Right to Economic Development

Even as he unveiled the plan, Prime Minister Singh made it clear that India will not give in to Western demands for mandatory cuts in greenhouse gas emissions. Singh described the NAPCC plan as one that "promotes [economic] development objectives while also yielding co-benefits of addressing climate change effectively. . . . [However, our] people have a right to economic and social development and to discard the ignominy of widespread poverty."[18]

While many Indians still face widespread poverty, the nation's economy is expanding almost as fast as China's—at a rate of around 9 percent a year. To put that in perspective, India's economy produced an extra $190 billion in wealth in 2006. That is nearly equal to the total economic output of Denmark. As Salil Tripathi, policy director for London's Institute for Human Rights and Business explains, this growth "was the equivalent of adding a rich country's economy to a very poor one."[19]

India's recent growth lifted 94 million people out of poverty, and these people have become new consumers. If each one installs a single 60-watt lightbulb in their home, India will need to build two giant 500-megawatt coal-burning power plants just to provide power to those bulbs. And most people have more than one lightbulb, in addition to televisions, microwaves, refrigerators, and other electronics. Consequently, India is planning to build dozens of coal-burning power plants by 2015.

"[China's economy] has to grow at a minimum of 8 percent a year or it will explode . . . because it will have so much unemployment and discontent the population will erupt."[20]

—Naya Chanda, economic analyst.

China's Emissions

While India's power needs are growing at a rapid pace, China's demand for electricity is even greater. To meet its needs, China is building the equivalent of three 500-megawatt coal-burning power plants every week. Researchers say that if China's electrical consumption continues at present rates, the nation's carbon dioxide production in 2030 will equal the entire world's CO_2 emissions in 2008.

The power is being used to drive an unprecedented expansion of manufacturing capabilities. For example, between 2000 and 2006 Chinese steel production more than tripled to 489 million tons (443.6 t) annually. This is more than twice the steel production of the United States and Japan combined. Much of the steel is being used to construct new cars. In 2006 the Chinese bought 7.2 million cars, 6 times as many as were sold in 1999.

New cars have increased demands for good roads, and China is also setting records for highway construction. These roads, along with China's growing network of luxury hotels, office and apartment buildings, parking garages, sewers, schools, and hospitals are all built with cement. Chinese cement is produced with vast amounts of cheap coal, used to heat kilns to 2,700°F (1,482°C). Cement production creates 5 percent of the world's total CO_2 emissions, and the Chinese are making half of all the cement produced on Earth every year. Not all the cement is used in China; some is exported to the United States, South Korea, and other nations. But wherever it is used, the carbon dioxide emissions from Chinese cement production alone is now equal to the total output of CO_2 from all sources in Great Britain.

Challenges in China

Despite its capitalist-style economy, China remains a Communist dictatorship. However, Chinese leaders have struck a bargain with citizens. If they work hard and make few demands for free speech or democracy, citizens can achieve the Chinese version of middle-class status or even become rich. However, experts say this bargain could collapse if the economy slows. As Asia economic analyst Naya Chanda explains, China's economy "has to grow at a minimum of 8 percent a year or it will explode . . . because it will have so much unemployment and discontent the population will erupt."[20]

With this reality, it is difficult for leaders in China to cut economic growth in order to reduce global warming. However, the

In 2008 China suffered from its most severe drought in 50 years. About 100,000 people were left without water. The drought affected wildlife and food harvests and forced many to relocate to urban areas.

Chinese understand they must devise ways to cope with global warming or they will face irreversible environmental disaster.

About half of China's huge territory is dry, or semiarid, like the American West. In 2008 China was already suffering from its most severe drought in half a century. The nation's largest freshwater lake, Poyang Lake, had shrunk 98 percent from its average size, destroying wildlife habitat and leaving 100,000 people without water.

The drought also affected food harvests throughout the country, creating shortages of staples such as wheat and rice. And researchers predict that if the drought continues in Northern China, by 2011 as many as 50 million people, many of them agricultural workers, will be forced to leave their homes because of water shortages and brutal sandstorms. These homeless people, called environmental refugees, will flock to overcrowded cities that are some of the most polluted urban environments on Earth.

Chinese planners have taken some steps to reduce global warming emissions, but balancing the demands of the economy and the needs of the environment has proved to be extremely difficult. Chanda compares the task to a bus speeding down the highway: "China's leaders are trying to replace the motor of that Chinese bus from a gas-guzzling polluter to a super-efficient hybrid—but they're trying to do it while the bus is still going 50 miles per hour."[21]

Wind, Sun, and Water

One of the most notable steps China has taken on its road to a greener economy concerns reforestation programs that were instituted in 1980. At that time only 12 percent of China was covered by forests, but by 2005 that number had grown to over 18 percent. That 6 percent growth is significant in a country as large as China. It equals an additional 348,000 square miles of forest, or 223 million acres (90 million ha), an area twice as big as California.

In more recent years China has invested heavily in renewable energy production. While two-thirds of the nation's electricity is generated by burning coal, China invested over $10 billion in solar, wind, and small hydropower projects in 2007.

Wind power holds the most promise for China, and the government has mandated that power companies produce a growing share of their electricity with wind. This has prompted more than 50 companies to begin producing wind turbines. These manufacturers are exporting their products to other countries, and China is expected to become the world's number one producer of wind turbines by 2010.

China's investment in solar power was displayed on the world stage during the 2008 Summer Olympics in Beijing. China had pledged to hold a "green Olympics" powered by renewable energy; and the Olympic Village, home to 12,000 athletes, trainers, and other personnel, was outfitted with solar showers and solar-powered street lights. In addition, the sloping roof of the National Indoor Stadium was covered with 1,100 solar panels.

China's Olympic solar project was largely for show. It was meant to convince the 4 billion viewers who tuned in to the Olympics that China was not the "Dirty Dragon," a nickname it has earned for its atrocious air pollution, toxic rivers, and extreme energy inefficiency. However, solar electricity is still in its infancy in China, where photovoltaic cells are mostly found in rural areas that are not connected to large power grids. Solar water heating is a different matter. About 10 percent of China's households, 40 million homes, produce hot water with solar heaters.

China has also become a world leader in hydroelectricity projects, power generated by water flowing through dams. One of the biggest projects, the Three Gorges Dam, was completed in October 2008. As the largest hydroelectric power station in the world, the $180 billion dam produces as much electricity as 45 average

Chinese workers assemble a wind turbine to be used at a wind farm in northwest China. The Chinese government has ordered the country's electricity producers to increase the use of wind power in meeting China's energy needs.

coal-burning plants. However, construction of the dam has been fraught with controversy because it flooded millions of acres, displaced 1.4 million people, and destroyed habitat for several endangered species.

Because of the problems associated with large-scale projects, Chinese planners are thinking small, building little hydroelectric dams that cause less environmental damage. These small hydro projects on rivers and streams provide power to rural areas without increasing carbon emissions.

Mixed Signals

With its growing use of renewable energy, China is expected to receive 21 percent of its electricity from solar and wind power by 2020. These projects are desperately needed because China's electricity use is the second highest in the world after the United States, and its demand for power is doubling about every six years.

While China is taking steps to produce cleaner electricity, officials have also stated that the government is committed to economic growth. This message was made clear when China unveiled the nation's first climate change action plan on June 3, 2007. The plan stated China's intentions to promote clean technologies, generate more renewable energy, improve energy efficiency, and restructure its economy to produce less pollution. Commenting on the plan, Ma Kai, director of China's National Development and Reform Commission, said, "Climate change is a challenge China must cope with to realize sustainable development. . . . Implementing a climate change containment policy may cost a fortune, but the cost will be even higher if we delay. Early action is imperative."[22]

China's action plan did not set specific goals for the reduction of global warming gases. But Chinese leaders have stressed that the need to provide food, shelter, and clothes for their citizens must come ahead of global warming concerns. And Ma pointed out that China produces much less CO_2, when measured per capita, or per person, than the populations in industrialized nations. For example, each American produces 4 times more emissions than

"Implementing a climate change containment policy may cost a fortune, but the cost will be even higher if we delay."[22]

—Ma Kai, director of China's National Development and Reform Commission.

each person in China, and 14 times more than each person in India. Challenging those who call China the Dirty Dragon or an environmental menace, Ma stated,

> I don't see how China can be labeled a menace. Compared to the industrialized countries, until recently China had low greenhouse gas emissions and its emissions are still relatively low in per capita terms. Rises in gross domestic product in China produce smaller hikes in carbon dioxide discharges than in other countries. This kind of talk is grossly exaggerated and unfair.[23]

Clean Development

No other developing nations produce emissions on the scale of China or India. For example, Mexico, the developing nation with the third most emissions, produces only about 1.4 percent of the world's total global warming gases. However, taken together, smaller developing nations create about 24 percent of all global emissions.

The lack of money and resources in most developing nations prevents governments from spending money to mitigate carbon dioxide and other global warming pollution. And it also leaves citizens extremely vulnerable to floods, high seas, droughts, and other phenomena traced to global warming. In order to alleviate these twin problems, industrial nations have implemented programs to reduce global warming gases in developing nations.

One such program, the Clean Development Mechanism (CDM), was put in place by the Kyoto Protocol. This program allows large polluters in industrialized nations to offset their emission by paying for environmental projects in developing nations. For example, if a large European steel company burns more coal than allowed in the Kyoto Protocol, the company can buy a credit from the CDM program. The money from this credit, along with millions collected on credits from other polluters, is used in developing nations on projects meant to reduce global warming.

Money from the CDM fund has been used for more than 1,000 projects since 2006. In the Philippines $70 million was

Global Warming and Failed States

The 2007 "National Security and the Threat of Climate Change" study, written by a dozen top U.S. military leaders, describes some of the ways climate change threatens the stability of developing nations. An excerpt of the study appears below.

> Climate change acts as a threat multiplier for instability in some of the most volatile regions of the world. Projected climate change will seriously exacerbate already marginal living standards in many Asian, African, and Middle Eastern nations, causing widespread political instability and the likelihood of failed states. Unlike most conventional security threats that involve a single entity acting in specific ways and points in time, climate change has the potential to result in multiple chronic conditions, occurring globally within the same time frame. Economic and environmental conditions in already fragile areas will further erode as food production declines, diseases increase, clean water becomes increasingly scarce, and large populations move in search of resources. Weakened and failing governments, with an already thin margin for survival, foster the conditions for internal conflicts, extremism, and movement toward increased authoritarianism and radical ideologies.

Gordon R. Sullivan et al., "National Security and the Threat of Climate Change," The CNA Corporation, 2007. http://securityandclimate.cna.org.

used in 17 projects designed to capture methane leaking from decomposing garbage in landfills. The captured methane is then burned as fuel in power plants. CDM money has also been used to plant millions of acres of forests in Mexico, Cambodia, Malaysia, and elsewhere. Other CDM projects include small hydroelectric projects and investments in solar, wind, biomass, and geothermal energy development.

While the CDM projects have helped offset global warming pollution, the program has its critics because three-fifths of the money is going to China. With a $1.2 trillion budget surplus, some experts say, the Chinese government can afford to fund its own projects. Instead, it has taken $3 billion of the $4.8 billion set aside by the CDM in 2006.

Despite the criticism, the CDM is providing a means for offsetting global warming gases. The projects also provide good employment opportunities in nations with extensive poverty. And in 2008 at least 4,200 new CDM projects were in the planning stages, most concerning renewable energy ventures. As in the past, China led the way with over 1,500 projects planned. Although the CDM program is imperfect, it allows a net reduction in emissions. And since climate change is a global problem, any reductions are welcomed.

FACTS

- Glaciers covering China's Tibet plateau are shrinking by 7 percent a year due to global warming.

- If global temperatures rise 3.6°F (1.98°C), rice production in India will fall 40 percent, leading to widespread food shortages.

- To stop drought-driven dust storms in northern China, the government will plant hardy grasses and shrubs on 250,000 square miles (64,750 ha) of desert by 2050.

- If sea levels rise three feet due to global warming, 75 to 150 million people will lose their homes in India, China, Vietnam, Bangladesh, and small Pacific island nations.

- In 2008 Mexico, the world's fourteenth largest CO_2 polluter, pledged to cut its global warming emissions in half by 2050.

How Should Developed Nations Respond?

The United States is the richest nation on Earth, and its economy is built on fossil fuels. As an industrial power-house, the United States long dominated the world in the production of steel, cars, airplanes, military hardware, electronics, and food.

The American consumer has been the top beneficiary of a society built on oil, coal, natural gas, and concrete. Americans live in a nation that has over 250 million registered motor vehicles and only 197 million licensed drivers. Ribbons of highway connect far-flung suburbs where strip malls, shopping centers, apartment buildings, gas stations, grocery stores, and motels fill in the spaces between Wal-Marts, McDonald's, Targets, and KFCs. To support this lifestyle, Americans consume more energy than anyone else on Earth. As the report *Lighting the Way* by the InterAcademy Council, a scientific research group, puts it:

> [The] average American consumes enough energy to meet the . . . needs of 100 people. . . . By comparison, China and India currently consume approximately 9–30 times less energy per person than the United States.[24]

This energy consumption is the reason why Americans, who make up only about 5 percent of the world's population, helped create over 22 percent of the world's global warming gases in 2008.

While the United States leads the way in carbon, methane, and nitrous oxide emissions, other developed nations also add to global warming. Japan creates about 5.6 percent of the CO_2 pumped into the atmosphere every year. Germany emits 3 percent of the world's emissions, the United Kingdom about 2.2 percent, and France 1.4 percent. Because people in these developed nations enjoy a higher standard of living than those in developing nations, it is widely agreed that solutions to global warming must focus on industrialized societies.

Expensive Gas, Small Cars

Germany, the United Kingdom, and France are part of the European Union (EU), a governing body composed of 27 countries. Other members of the EU include Italy, Spain, Poland, Ireland, Sweden, the Netherlands, and Austria. Collectively, the 495 million people of the European Union produce 14 percent of the worlds' global warming gases.

The average citizen of the European Union uses about half as much energy as the average American. During the past several decades, while Americans were buying record numbers of gas-guzzling SUVs, European governments slowed oil consumption by placing high taxes on gasoline. These taxes mean that Europeans have been spending $6 to $9 for a gallon of gasoline since the 1980s. Much of the tax money has been used to pay for highly efficient public transportation systems, including high-speed rail. The so-called bullet trains of this system travel over 125 miles (201km) per hour and connect Paris, Brussels, Amsterdam, Cologne, and other cities.

High gas prices also mean that many Europeans drive small, lightweight vehicles, such as the Ford Fiesta ECOnetic, which gets 65 miles per gallon (27.5 km per L), as well as Smart Cars and Minis that go 45 miles (64 km) on a gallon of gas. Unlike Americans, Europeans who purchase new cars also learn how much CO_2 they are pumping into the air. Since 2002 every new car sold in the EU bears a government mandated "Global Warming Performance Label." This large window sticker warns potential buyers that "CO_2 is the main greenhouse gas responsible for global warming"[25] and states how many pounds of CO_2 the car produces per mile traveled. For example, a car that gets 20 miles per gallon (8.4km per L) emits 20 pounds (9 kg) of CO_2 for every gallon (3.8 L) of gasoline burned.

"[The] average American consumes enough energy to meet the . . . needs of 100 people."[24]

—The InterAcademy Council, a scientific research group.

A car that gets 60 miles per gallon (25.4 km per L) produces one-third as much CO_2.

European Emissions Trading Scheme

Automobiles generate around 25 percent of carbon dioxide emissions in Europe, while power plants and industrial facilities create about twice as much. To reduce pollution from these sources, the EU created the Emissions Trading Scheme (ETS), which went into effect on January 1, 2005.

The ETS, based on emissions reductions outlined in the Kyoto Protocol, is the largest multinational cap-and-trade system in the world. The scheme sets a limit, or cap, for every nation concerning the amount of global warming gases it is allowed to generate. This number is adjusted downward by about 5 percent annually so that an overall reduction occurs year after year.

To achieve its goals the ETS regulates pollution from over 12,000 facilities in 25 countries. Each one of these steel mills,

A new high-speed train arrives at Italy's central rail station in Milan. The European Union has made high-speed rail a priority, taxing gasoline to pay for its development and providing Europeans with a dependable and energy-efficient option for travel.

cement producers, oil refineries, glass producers, electric utilities, paper mills, and other manufacturing plants is issued one credit for each ton of pollution it is allowed to produce. Those who pollute less than the set limits can "bank" their credit and use it to pollute more the following year. Polluters can also sell their credits to those who exceed the limits. However, if large polluters are unable to buy spare credits because none are available, they are given heavy fines of about $130 per excess ton of CO_2. These polluters must also make reductions the following year equal to the amount they exceeded.

The objective of the ETS is for the European Union nations to produce 8 percent less CO_2 than they did in 1990. Regulators hope to achieve this goal by 2012. However, environmentalists have leveled criticism at this ambitious program. One problem is that so many excess credits are available that they are selling for only about $15, considerably less than the $130 per ton fine charged by the ETS. In addition, large industrial polluters have been able to exaggerate their emissions in order to receive more permits. Even with low-credit trading prices this has allowed the biggest polluters to make billions in profits by simply selling their excess credits on the market. In Great Britain alone, windfall profits from overgenerous ETS credits earned the most polluting industries $1.7 billion in 2006. Kevin Smith, environmental researcher for the Carbon Trade Watch organization, is a strong critic of the trade scheme:

> Given all we know about the link between pollution and climate change, such a massive public concession to dirty industries borders on the obscene. . . . Carbon trading isn't an effective response; emissions have to be reduced across the board without elaborate [escape] clauses for the biggest polluters. . . . Market-based mechanisms such as carbon trading are an elaborate shell-game . . . that distracts us from the fact that there is no viable "business as usual" scenario.[26]

Despite the criticism, emissions by the EU nations dipped 8 percent below 1990s levels in 2007. This was mainly due to large cuts by Germany, Finland, and the Netherlands, countries that have installed thousands of wind turbines and utilized other means to generate renewable energy.

In 2008 the EU promised to reduce total emissions by another 20 percent by 2020. This disappointed environmentalists who were hoping for a 30 percent target. The targeted reductions also enraged industrialists who will be forced to pay more for the right to pollute. Members of the German Cement Industry trade group calculated their costs would rise $1.4 billion if they were forced to pay for extra ETS permits. Cement makers fear the added burden will give foreign rivals a competitive edge. This would force German cement makers, who abide by strict environmental rules, to shut down and move to nations which have few environmental regulations. As one unnamed cement factory manager commented, "We will simply move our cement operation to Ukraine. Then there won't be any trading here, nothing will be produced here anymore—the lights will simply go out here."[27]

The Global Warming Hoax

The United States has no cap-and-trade system like the European Union, and in 2007 the United States produced a record 8 billion tons (7.25 billion t) of carbon dioxide, methane, and nitrous oxide. This number was 16 percent higher than 1990 levels. Experts say the increase over the years is largely due to the fact that nearly half of all vehicles sold in the United States between 1995 and 2005 were pickup trucks or SUVs. These larger vehicles produce an average of 43 percent more global warming pollutants than cars. However, the political will to lower American CO_2 emissions has been lacking.

In the United States powerful industries such as oil, coal, and auto companies spend hundreds of millions of dollars to influence the political process. For example, in 2008 the Big Three automakers, General Motors, Ford, and Chrysler, gave more than $15 million to senators and congressman. They also spent $50 million on lobbyists, people who are paid to pressure legislatures and other government officials. This money has no doubt been a good investment for the Big Three. Un-

"Carbon trading isn't an effective response; emissions have to be reduced across the board without elaborate [escape] clauses for the biggest polluters."[26]

—Kevin Smith, environmental researcher for the Carbon Trade Watch.

Dissent over Global Warming

On December 11, 2008, Oklahoma senator James Inhofe released a 231-page report entitled, "U.S. Senate Minority Report: More than 650 International Scientists Dissent over Man-Made Global Warming Claims." The report features the views of scientists who question claims about global warming. The beginning of the report features selected comments from individual scientists. Some of their comments appear below.

"I am a skeptic. . . . Global warming has become a new religion."

—Ivar Giaever, Nobel Prize winner for Physics.

"So far, real measurements give no ground for concern about a catastrophic future warming."

—Scientist Jarl R. Ahlbeck, a chemical engineer at Abo Akademi University in Finland.

"Anyone who claims that the debate is over and the conclusions are firm has a fundamentally un-scientific approach to one of the most momentous issues of our time."

—Solar physicist Pal Brekke, senior adviser to the Norwegian Space Centre in Oslo.

"It is a blatant lie put forth in the media that makes it seem there is only a fringe of scientists who don't buy into anthropogenic global warming."

—U.S. Government Atmospheric Scientist Stanley B. Goldenberg of the Hurricane Research Division of NOAA.

James Inhofe, "U.S. Senate Minority Report: More Than 650 International Scientists Dissent over Man-Made Global Warming Claims," U.S. Senate Environment and Public Works Committee, December 11, 2008. www.epw.senate.gov.

til 2008 American automobile manufacturers successfully repelled 20 years of congressional efforts to force automakers to redesign cars and trucks to achieve better gas mileage.

The oil industry is also a major donor to lobbyists and politicians, spending a record $83 million in 2007 to convince lawmakers to support its interests. One of the chief beneficiaries of the oil company money is Oklahoma senator James Inhofe, who has received over $1 million from the oil and gas industry.

Inhofe dismisses the scientific consensus that says climate change is a result of human activities. When he became chairman of the Senate Committee on Environment and Public Works in 2003, Inhofe made headlines when he inferred that global warming science was fraudulent: "With all of the hysteria, all of the fear, all of the phony science, could it be that man-made global warming is the greatest hoax ever perpetrated on the American people? It sure sounds like it."[28]

In 2007 Inhofe lost his chairmanship to California Democrat Barbara Boxer, an environmental champion who believes in the accuracy of global warming science.

"A Liberal Cause"

Environmentalists, climatologists, and researchers have long rejected the contention that global warming science is a hoax. Many believe that Inhofe was following a policy devised by powerful political consultant Frank Luntz in 2002. In a report entitled *Winning the Global Warming Debate*, written for the Republican National Committee, Luntz stated that a majority of voters believe that scientists are not in agreement concerning global warming. Luntz advised Republicans to emphasize this uncertainty, writing "Should the public come to believe that the scientific issues are settled, their views about global warming will change accordingly. Therefore, we need to continue to make the lack of scientific certainty a primary issue."[29]

This type of thinking guided the George W. Bush Administration from 2001 until 2008. As Surgeon General Richard H. Carmona testified before Congress, top administration officials dismissed global warming as a "liberal cause"[30] to be treated as a political, not a scientific, issue. Bush appointed officials from the coal, oil, chemical, logging, and automobile industries to top environmental posts. For example, Philip Cooney was made chief of staff of the Council on Environmental Quality (CEQ), a department within the White House that manages federal environmental programs in the United States. Cooney was not a scientist but a lawyer who previously

Smart cars are on display outside a factory in France. Europeans have been driving small, lightweight vehicles for years. The Smart car, which gets 45 miles per gallon, was recently introduced in the United States along with other energy-efficient autos.

worked as a lobbyist for the American Petroleum Institute (API), a trade association for the oil and natural gas industry.

At API, Cooney led the oil industry's fight against limits on greenhouse gases. At the CEQ, the former lobbyist created controversy when the department's internal documents revealed that he was editing reports written by panels of scientists, rewriting sentences and crossing out paragraphs to downplay the projected effects of global warming. After the story was picked up by the *New York Times* and covered on the television show *60 Minutes* Cooney admitted, "We'd take the text from EPA [the Environmental

New Energy for America

In January 2009 President Barack Obama and Vice President Joe Biden released their "New Energy for America" plan to address global climate change. The plan is posted on the White House Web site. An excerpt follows.

President Obama and Vice President Biden have a comprehensive plan to invest in alternative and renewable energy, end our addiction to foreign oil, address the global climate crisis and create millions of new jobs. The Obama-Biden comprehensive New Energy for America plan will:

- Help create 5 million new jobs by strategically investing $150 billion over the next 10 years to catalyze private efforts to build a clean energy future.
- Within 10 years save more oil than we currently import from the Middle East and Venezuela combined.
- Put 1 million Plug-in Hybrid cars—cars that can get up to 150 miles per gallon—on the road by 2015, cars that we will work to make sure are built here in America.
- Ensure 10 percent of our electricity comes from renewable sources by 2012, and 25 percent by 2025.
- Implement an economy-wide cap-and-trade program to reduce greenhouse gas emissions 80 percent by 2050.

The White House, "The Agenda: Energy and the Environment," January 2009. www.whitehouse.gov.

Protection Agency], and then we'd add a sentence like, 'We don't really know if this is really happening.' So we tried to do it, but I can see now that we made a total mess of it."[31] Cooney was forced to resign in 2005 and was immediately hired to an executive position at the ExxonMobile Corporation.

Cooney's departure did little to reduce the power of the fossil fuels industries in the Senate. Two months after his resignation, Congress passed the Energy Policy Act with strong support from the Bush administration. The bill was considered a disaster by environmentalists because it contained $6 billion in subsidies for oil and gas production at a time when oil companies were reaping record profits. Another $9 billion was included for coal producers while only $500 million was dedicated to renewable energy projects. The bill also eliminated regulations that slowed the construction of coal-fired power plants, allowing utilities to begin construction on dozens of new generators that will add global warming gases to the atmosphere.

Cap and Trade in the United States

Some senators attempted to add an amendment to the Energy Policy Act of 2005 that would establish a mandatory cap-and-trade system to limit greenhouse gas emissions. This was rejected, however. The following year, seven separate bills were introduced that would promote renewable technologies to reduce greenhouse gas emissions or establish a cap-and-trade system. These bills were also rejected. Commenting on the proposals, James Edwards, secretary of energy during the Reagan administration, stated that cap and trade would be "an industrial manager's nightmare [that would] destroy industry in America."[32] Similar bills failed to pass in 2007 and 2008. However, in December 2007 President Bush signed into law the "Energy Independence and Security Act," which mandated the first increase in car fuel economy in 32 years. This bill raised the average fuel economy of all cars produced in the United States to 35 miles per gallon (14.7 km per L), up from 27.5 miles per gallon (11.7 km per L).

State and City Initiatives

Lack of action in Washington on the climate issue has prompted 28 states to implement mandatory programs to reduce greenhouse gas emissions. By addressing these problems the states have become what are called policy laboratories, experimenting with initiatives that, if successful, might someday serve as models for federal programs.

"Could it be that man-made global warming is the greatest hoax ever perpetrated on the American people?" [28]

—James Inhofe, Oklahoma senator.

States are attacking climate change in several sectors, but some measures have been opposed by the federal government. For example, California passed legislation requiring all new cars sold in the state to reduce CO_2 emissions 30 percent by 2016. However, this measure was opposed by the Big Three because they did not want to manufacture cars specifically for California, although it is the nation's biggest car market.

The Bush administration's Environmental Protection Agency (EPA) denied California the right to regulate auto emissions, saying the issue was a federal matter. However, 16 other states joined with California to fight the EPA ruling in court. In 2007 two federal courts ruled in favor of the state restrictions, but the EPA continued to refuse California permission to regulate tailpipe CO_2.

Beyond fighting lawsuits in federal court, states have joined together to coordinate efforts to lower greenhouse emissions. One of these state organizations, the West Coast Governors' Global Warming Initiative, has plans to improve the performance of state fleet vehicles, purchase hybrid vehicles that get over 40 miles per gallon (17 km per L), and force electric utilities to purchase renewable energy. The three states behind the initiative, California, Oregon, and Washington, also plan to incorporate aggressive energy efficiency measures in state building codes to reduce energy consumption by at least 15 percent by 2015.

City governments have also initiated measures to lower their carbon footprints. Much of this planning revolves around what is called smart growth, an urban planning method that concentrates growth in the center of a city. By building offices, entertainment venues, apartments, houses, and parks in centralized neighborhoods, smart growth advocates are able to promote public transportation, bicycle use, and pedestrian-friendly communities that reduce reliance on private automobiles. This is seen as an alternative to urban sprawl where houses are built far from cities, forcing residents to rely on cars to get to work, schools, and shops.

Seattle mayor Greg Nickels is a leading proponent of smart growth. In 2005, in order to advance the goals of the Kyoto Protocol, Nickels founded the organization "Cities for Climate Protec-

"There is already widespread harm . . . occurring from climate change. This is not a problem for our children and our grandchildren." [33]

—John Holdren, director of the White House Office of Science and Technology.

tion." By 2008, 980 U.S. cities and towns had joined the group in which smart growth planning is seen as a major way to reduce emissions.

"Science Holds the Key to Our Survival"

In 2009 the Barack Obama administration began to reverse the Bush policies on global warming. Obama, who favors a cap-and-trade system to reduce CO_2 emissions, appointed Harvard physicist and climate change expert John Holdren as director of the White House Office of Science and Technology, which deals with global warming issues. Holdren, a former president of the American Association for the Advancement of Science, made clear his view that global warming is already an imminent threat to the planet: "There is already widespread harm . . . occurring from climate change. This is not a problem for our children and our grandchildren."[33] When making the appointment, Obama emphasized that he believes global warming is a scientific, not a political, problem: "Today, more

Harvard physicist John Holdren is the director of the White House Office of Science and Technology, the office charged with handling global warming issues. He has made it clear that global warming and climate change are already imminent threats.

than ever before, science holds the key to our survival as a planet and our security and prosperity as a nation. It's time we once again put science at the top of our agenda. . . . [The scientific process is] about ensuring that facts and evidence are never twisted nor obscured by politics nor ideology."[34]

While many environmentalists and global warming scientists were cheered by Obama's words, some believe that it may be impossible to stop climate change. In 2008 a study by researcher Roger Pielke Jr., atmospheric scientist Tom Wigley, and economist Christopher Green said that reducing global warming emissions will be much more challenging than society has been led to believe. In the article "Dangerous Assumptions" published in *Nature*, the scientists state that people are expecting the introduction of new carbon-neutral energy sources to help lower CO_2 emissions. But in order to achieve a 50 percent reduction in carbon emissions by 2060, car companies would have to build 2 billion cars that get at least 60 miles per gallon (25.4 km per L). Meanwhile, all other cars would have to be removed from the road. Additional requirements would include bringing one million wind turbines on line and doubling global nuclear capacity to replace coal plants. Coal power plants that remained in operation would have to capture and store carbon emissions underground in caves. But the technology to do so does not exist.

So even as scientists call for a 50 to 80 percent reduction in CO_2 emissions by the end of the twenty-first century, the goal is extremely daunting and may prove impossible. Al Gore has compared this to the public mobilization required to fight World War II combined with the scientific knowledge that was harnessed to put a man on the moon. However, those tasks were undertaken with very little political or public opposition, whereas reducing global warming gases will require nearly everyone in industrial society to reduce consumption, pay more for power, and make other lifestyle sacrifices for decades. Whether this can happen is a matter of speculation.

FACTS

- Climate change fueled by pollution from the world's wealthiest countries is expected to have the most impact in the world's poorest countries.

- The five-passenger Ford Fiesta ECOnetic, which gets 65 miles per gallon (27.5 km per L), is sold only in Europe. Ford has no plans to sell the fuel-efficient vehicle in the United States because it runs on diesel fuel, which is unpopular with American motorists.

- In 2007 the American Enterprise Institute, a think tank funded by ExxonMobil, offered $10,000 to any scientist who would write an article disputing the facts surrounding global warming.

- The Energy Policy Act of 2005 required the federal government to derive 7.5 percent of its electricity from renewable sources by 2013.

- In 2007 San Francisco became the first city in the United States to offer programs to offset CO_2 by funding green initiatives such as planting trees and reducing emissions from traffic.

How Should Business and Industry Respond?

Climate change became an environmental and political issue in the 1980s. But until very recently, the majority of business leaders in the United States doubted the need for urgency in responding to global warming. They said the science behind global warming was not certain and any attempt to force them to lower emissions would result in higher prices, unemployment, and financial disaster for the United States. That attitude is still prevalent among some businesspeople, but a change in thinking has occurred in the past decade.

Some have come to believe that climate change may affect the survival of their enterprises. For example, those who are in the tourism business fear stronger hurricanes and rising sea levels will destroy scenic beaches from California to the Caribbean. And melting glaciers, forest fires, and droughts might shut down ski resorts and campgrounds in mountain regions. Such conditions would also affect the agricultural business, the forestry and paper products industries, real estate sales, and offshore energy development.

The insurance industry has been one of the loudest voices in the global warming debate. These companies are already paying out record settlements to people whose homes and businesses have been destroyed by increasingly numerous and violent hurricanes. Hurricane Katrina alone cost the insurance industry over $55 billion.

Analysts of the insurance business believe climate change is increasing property damage claims at an average rate of 2 to 4 percent annually. This means that within 25 years, insurance companies could be dealing with twice the number of claims they are paying today. Commenting on the risk, a spokesperson for insurance giant AIG stated: "Climate change is increasingly recognized as an ongoing, significant global environmental problem with potential risks to the global economy and ecology, and to human health and well-being.[35]

Regulatory Risk

Corporations that produce excessive CO_2 emissions in the United States face a risk that has nothing to do with weather-related catastrophes. Fossil fuels industries, cement makers, and others face what is called regulatory risk. This is the possibility that governments will impose new rules and regulations concerning global warming gases. Because of the costs associated with implementing new regulations, many businesses oppose government mandates. However, many corporate officers see it as inevitable that they will soon have to deal with a cap-and-trade system and other regulations.

In a 2006 poll of businesspeople conducted by the Pew Center on Climate Change, all respondents said they expected to see some sort of national greenhouse gas regulations in the near future. Seventeen percent believed new rules will probably take effect before 2010, while 84 percent said regulations will be in place before 2015. A smaller number believed the regulations would be enacted between 2015 and 2020. In order to lessen the expenses associated with regulatory risk, some companies are already taking steps to lower their emissions so that the transition to a cap-and-trade system will be smoother.

Companies benefit from lowering their carbon footprints before the federal government requires them to do so. According to the Pew Center on Global Climate Change:

> Their motivations include gaining a head start over competitors in learning what climate strategies work, preparing to respond rapidly once regulations do take effect, and

"Many companies recognize that acting early to reduce emissions is an important way to gain credibility and influence among lawmakers as they consider what policies will work best."[36]

—Pew Center on Global Climate Change.

better managing the costs of reducing their emissions over time. In addition, many companies recognize that acting early to reduce emissions is an important way to gain credibility and influence among lawmakers as they consider what policies will work best.[36]

Better Gas Mileage Lowers Emissions

Global warming is largely caused by burning fossil fuels, and in the United States 20 percent of all CO_2 emissions come from cars and trucks. With California and other states attempting to reduce tailpipe emissions by 30 percent through new regulations, the race is on to develop vehicles that use little or no gasoline and therefore pollute less.

Major auto companies have designed three types of cars meant to wean motorists from gasoline. The cars run on alternative fuels or batteries, or are hybrid electric vehicles (HEVs) that run on a combination of gasoline and battery power. Some have appeared only as futuristic concept cars. Others, like the Toyota Prius and Honda hybrid models, have been on the road since 2000.

Hybrids have small gasoline motors that work in tandem with batteries to provide 45 to 60 miles per gallon (19 km to 96.6 km per L). This means that hybrids produce about one-half to one-third less CO_2 than an average American car. These cars became very popular after gas prices topped $4 a gallon in 2008, the year Toyota produced its one millionth Prius.

Car companies are hoping to improve on hybrids by developing a new generation of cars called plug-in hybrid electric vehicles (PHEV). These cars are similar to HEVs, but their batteries can be recharged in any electrical outlet. And unlike HEVs, they do not rely on their gasoline motors except on journeys over 100 miles (161 km). Since the average commuter drives less than 40 miles (64.4 km) per day, some motorists would never have to stop at a filling station.

If a PHEV is charged with electricity generated from solar, wind, hydroelectric, or nuclear power, it will add zero CO_2 to the atmosphere. However, since 50 percent of the electricity in the United States comes from coal power, many PHEV owners will

still contribute to global warming when they plug in their car for a charge. But electric cars still pollute less than gasoline-powered vehicles. As Martin Eberhard, founder of electric vehicle company Tesla Motors says, "if you do the math, you'll find that an electric car, even if you use coal to make electricity, produces less pollution per mile than burning gasoline in the best gasoline-powered car."[37]

The gasoline-electric hybrid engine (pictured) that powers Toyota's Prius runs more efficiently than conventional car engines. Because it uses less gasoline, it also emits fewer pollutants.

Electric Cars

Tesla Motors is a small company producing sleek sports cars that run on batteries, achieve speeds of over 120 miles (193 km) per hour, and sell for more than $100,000. However, several major car companies are planning more affordable electric vehicles (EVs).

General Motors is expected to begin production of the Chevrolet Volt in 2010. This car is an electric vehicle powered by a lithium-ion battery pack that can go about 40 miles (64.4 km) before the batteries need recharging. However, the Volt will be equipped with what GM calls a "range-extending"[38] gasoline-powered engine. This motor will charge the battery pack and generate electricity

Looking to Mother Nature for Car Design

Steve Fambro, founder of the Aptera hybrid car company, discusses how he came up with the design of the super-efficient Aptera 2e:

> Open up any book on automotive design and styling. Look at how they begin drawing a new concept vehicle. They almost always start with a rectangle!!!! . . . That's crazy! . . . Why is it crazy? Because about 65% of the gasoline we use as a country is used by our cars just to push the air out of the way due to their *styling*, or more correctly, the high aerodynamic drag due to their styling. . . .

> This understanding of designing for low drag is fundamental to Aptera's core. . . . Now, it is no secret that the 2e is streamlined just as many birds and fish are. There is a very close connection here: nature abhors inefficiency, as does Aptera. Birds and fish have evolved for millennia to expend the least amount of energy while moving through the air or water as swiftly as possible. So in many ways, Aptera looked to Mother Nature and simply re-discovered what has evolved for millennia.

Steve Fambro, "The Founders Mind: Thoughts from the Pen of Steve Fambro," Aptera, November 19, 2008. www.aptera.com.

to propel the car for longer trips. GM says the car is not a hybrid because it can run without the gasoline motor. Instead, the Volt is called an "Extended Range Electric Vehicle" or EREV.

Mitsubishi is building an all electric vehicle, the iMiEV, with no gas motor onboard. iMiEV stands for In-wheel Motor Innovative Electric Vehicle. It is so named because the battery-powered electric motors that propel the vehicle are mounted behind each wheel. This system is beneficial because the car does not require a traditional transmission, driveshaft, and other equipment that add weight while pushing up the cost of a vehicle. With a lithium-ion battery pack the iMiEV can travel about 85 miles (136.8 km) at 55 miles (88.5 km) per hour. When plugged into a 220-volt outlet the car can recharge in 7 hours. It can also be recharged using a standard 110-volt outlet, although that takes twice as long. The company is also developing a quick-charge system that will allow the car to charge 80 percent in 3 hours. The car will go on sale in Japan in 2009, but it will be several more years before it can be sold in the United States since the body needs to be redesigned to meet federal side-impact crash standards.

While major auto producers are planning a new generation of electric cars, for the first time in nearly 100 years small companies are also designing and building cars. In 2008 at least 15 new electric car companies were developing EVs based on different consumer needs.

In 2008 Steve Frambo, a biotech engineer in Carlsbad, California, began producing a three-wheel, lightweight car called Aptera, with an interior made from recycled plastic bottles. Aptera is very aerodynamic, which means it is designed to have very little air resistance as it moves down the road. This allows the hybrid Aptera to go 300 miles (483 km) on a gallon (3.8 L) of gas, while the all-electric version can achieve 100 miles (161km) on a single charge that costs an estimated 50 cents. Both models have a top speed of 95 miles (153 km) per hour. The Aptera also comes equipped with solar roof panels that assist the heating and cooling systems.

Investing in Clean Tech and Green Tech

Some of the financing for the EV start-up companies has been provided by forward-thinking lenders that invest in environmentally friendly businesses called clean tech or green tech. For example, Aptera was given loans and grants by Google.org, a charitable arm of the Internet search engine company Google. The charity was set up with a $1 billion grant and a mandate to solve problems related to poverty, disease, and global warming. In 2008 one of its first projects was to provide money

"If you do the math, you'll find that an electric car, even if you use coal to make electricity, produces less pollution per mile than burning gasoline in the best gasoline-powered car."[37]

—Martin Eberhard, founder of Tesla Motors, an electric vehicle company.

to engineers and start-up car companies to develop an ultra-fuel-efficient plug-in hybrid car that runs on ethanol fuel, electricity, or gasoline.

Google is one of many companies taking an interest in clean-tech transportation. According to the London research firm New Energy Finance, investors (called venture capitalists) provided a record $117 billion to alternative energy companies in 2007. The money went to start-ups that are producing solar panels, biofuels, wind generators, and superefficient cars. Venture capitalists believe that money put into these companies could initiate major societal changes as important as the computer revolution of the 1980s and 1990s. As Brian Dumaine, editor of *Fortune Small Business* explains:

> The same venture capitalists who provided money to create the computer industry and the Internet . . . believe green tech will be to the energy industry what . . . the Internet has been to traditional media—a disruptive force that destroys old business models and ushers in . . . new, better technologies [that] push out the old. The creation of new green businesses can happen with conglomerates such as Toyota, GE, and Sharp, but innovation is much more likely to come from small companies because change is much harder in large organizations.[39]

Dumaine believes that the new wave of green tech companies will create millions of jobs and will generate more wealth than the Internet boom of the 1990s.

Plug-In Start-Up

A start-up company called Better Place in Palo Alto, California, hopes to disrupt the way major oil companies have been doing business for nearly a century. In November 2008 Better Place founder Shai Agassi announced that his company planned to install thousands of electric car charging stations in San Francisco, Hawaii, Israel, Denmark, and Australia. Better Place stations allow motorists to quickly charge their electric cars while they are parked. They also allow EV drivers to pull into special garages where their depleted battery packs can be quickly exchanged for fully charged units. Agassi, a former senior executive at software giant SAP, believes such stations are necessary so that people will be inspired to buy electric cars. As he told the *Los Angeles Times*, "You cannot put electric cars on the road without infrastructure [to charge them], just as you can't drive cars without gas stations."[40]

Agassi, who raised $200 million for Better Place, also wants to change the way automobiles are sold, basing his sales model on the cell phone business, which provides phones for little or no money and charges users for service. Instead of someone buying an electric car and paying for the charge, subscribers to a Better Place would receive electric cars for a low cost if they committed to buying their electricity from Agassi's company. That way, his company would receive revenue for every mile driven by customers. As he explains, "If Ford got 1 cent per mile for every Ford car on the road, Ford would get $10 billion a year."[41]

Agassi devised the idea for Better Place when asked to deliver a presentation at the World Economic Forum on how to make the world a better place by 2020. His project was "how to convert an entire country from oil by the market, not by [government] edict and not as a science project."[42]

"The creation of new green businesses can happen with conglomerates . . . but innovation is much more likely to come from small companies because change is much harder in large organizations."[39]

—Brian Dumaine, editor of *Fortune Small Business.*

What Any Business Can Do

A business does not have to try to change the world in order to help the environment. Experts say conservation is the easiest and fastest way to lower emissions, and any company can take steps to lower its carbon footprint while saving money at the same time. For example, when computers are left on all the time, they continue to draw power. However, if computers are put on sleep mode during the day and shut down at night, the savings can be significant. Using sleep mode saves $25 to $75 per desktop computer every year on power bills. Turning a computer off at night saves $40 per unit. And those who switch to laptops save even more as they use 90 percent less energy than desktop models. This action also reduces global warming gas emissions. For example, when the state of Massachusetts ordered its office workers to use sleep mode or shut down their computers, the state saved $2 million a year and reduced carbon emissions by more than 5,000 tons (4,536t) annually.

E-Commuting

Some companies have found that the best way to save energy is to have their employees work from home, a policy called telecommuting or e-commuting. The average American adult spends one hour a day driving to and from work and while traveling 8,000 miles (13,000 km) commuting every year. But those who work from home avoid a daily drive on traffic-choked roads, which saves them time and money while they help the environment. A study by the Telework Coalition, which promotes e-commuting, found that if 32 million Americans worked from home only one day a week they would collectively avoid driving 1.2 billion miles (1.9 billion km) a year. This would prevent 68 million gallons (258 million L) of gasoline from being burned and save the telecommuters about $136 million in fuel expenses. In addition, if these cars were parked that one extra day every week, 1.3 billion pounds (600 million kg) of CO_2 would not be pumped into the atmosphere.

Airplane travel is another expensive contributor to global warming. An average 1,200-mile round-trip business excursion (1,931 km) in the United States costs a company $2,000. In addition, each traveler contributes about 1,100 pounds (499 kg) of CO_2 to the atmosphere. If the company chose instead to hold a Web conference, with employees tuning in with their computers, it would save thousands of dollars while creating very little atmospheric pollution.

The telecommunications giant British Telecom has been using video conferencing to its advantage. By replacing 900,000 face-to-face meetings in one year with e-conferencing, the company saved $198 million in travel expenses and 107,000 tons (97,000 t) in CO_2 emissions.

Flying on Vegetable Oil

Although airline flights produce only 3 percent of man-made CO_2 emissions, jet engines produce nitrous oxide, another greenhouse

"You cannot put electric cars on the road without infrastructure [to charge them], just as you can't drive cars without gas stations." [40]

—Shai Agassi, founder of Better Place, builder of electric car charging stations.

gas. Airplanes also emit sulfur dioxide, soot, and water vapor, which doubles their total warming effect on the climate.

One airline, Virgin Atlantic Airways, is trying to reduce its carbon footprint by switching its jets to biofuel, a fuel mixture made from 20 to 50 percent vegetable oil. British billionaire Richard Branson, who owns Virgin Atlantic, has gone beyond experimenting with a less polluting fuel. In 2006 Branson pledged to commit all airline profits over the next 10 years, an estimated $3 billion, to

In 2006, Virgin Atlantic Airways owner Richard Branson announced that his airline would give approximately $3 billion to research and development of alternative energy sources. The airline is also switching its jets to a biofuel mixture made with vegetable oil.

Business Solutions

A 2007 report "Climate Change 101: Business Solutions," by the Pew Center on Global Climate Change listed the changes some major corporations are making to help society lower greenhouse gas emissions:

> In June 2006 Dupont and BP announced a partnership to develop, market, and produce butanol, a new type of biofuel potentially superior to ethanol in terms of energy content, reduction in greenhouse gases, and ease of integration into existing fuel distribution infrastructure. . . .
>
> DTE Energy operates 29 landfill gas recovery projects at sites across the United States. These projects recover methane, a greenhouse gas, and convert it into pipeline-quality gas for producing steam or electricity. . . .
>
> From 1990 to 2002, IBM's energy conservation measures resulted in . . . avoiding approximately 7.8 million tons of carbon dioxide emissions and saving the company $729 million in reduced energy costs.
>
> Alcoa has saved hundreds of millions of dollars by reducing the electricity required to produce a ton of aluminum by 7.5 percent over the last 20 years.

Pew Center on Global Climate Change, "Climate Change 101: Business Strategies," 2008. www.pew climate.org.

combat global warming. The money will be used for research and development of alternative energy sources. Commenting on the plan, Branson stated: "Our generation has inherited an incredibly beautiful world from our parents and they from their parents. We must not be the generation responsible for irreversibly damaging the environment."[43]

While some laud Branson's goals, biofuels, which are largely produced with palm oil, present some environmental problems. Energy companies joining the biofuels boom are investing billions to plant oil palm plantations in Indonesia, Malaysia, and Thailand. In doing so they cleared vast tracts of rain forest, an estimated 100,000 acres (40,500 ha) a day. And unlike the native forests they replace, palm plantations have a negative environmental impact because they use high volumes of water and are treated with great quantities of pesticides.

The biofuel boom elevated oil palm to the world's number one fruit crop, ahead of bananas. But Simone Lovera, manager of the environmental organization Global Forest Coalition, calls the crop "deforestation diesel."[44] In addition, producing enough fuel

A tractor hauls palm tree parts on a palm plantation in Malaysia. Palm oil is one of the products commonly used in making biofuels. Environmentalists fear that too many forests are being cleared to make room for palm plantations.

The Sonoran Desert, located in Arizona and California, could someday be used to produce enough biofuel to replace all of the petroleum used in the United States.

for a modern airline company is impossible because of the vast acreage needed to grow the crops. As Jos Dings, director of the European Federation of Transport and the Environment, stated, "If Virgin would power its entire fleet with biofuel, it would have to use about half of [Great Britain's farm] land."[45] With airline flights expected to double to 9 billion a year by 2025, biofuel critics say the only way to significantly cut airline greenhouse gas emissions is for people to take fewer flights.

Despite his detractors, Branson understands that palm oil is not the greenest fuel. That is why he is working with Boeing Company, the world's leading manufacturer of commercial airliners, to develop an unlikely biofuel source. Researchers believe that by 2015, jet airplanes will be fueled with algae because some species contain over 50 percent oil. Growing these types of algae for biofuel would not require valuable farmland. The organisms can be grown in wastewater at sewage treatment plants or in seawater piped into algae farms located in desolate desert areas. Using the Sonoran Desert in Arizona and California as an example, scientists estimate that about 12 percent of the desert could someday produce enough biofuel to replace all of the petroleum used in the United States.

Resistance Remains

Today, countless companies are working to reduce their global warming emissions. But resistance remains in some important industries, especially the big oil companies that have dominated American business for a century. Companies such as ExxonMobile, Conoco-Phillips, and Chevron have invested trillions of dollars over the years in pipelines, oil refineries, tankers, and gas stations. And people worldwide continue to burn 40,000 gallons (152,000 L) of gas every second of every day, which provides the oil companies with record profits year after year. ExxonMobile alone made $40.6 billion in 2007. With numbers like that it is not hard to see why an unnamed investment banker told Dumaine, "We're going to keep looking for oil and building coal plants unless people want to stop driving their cars and live in dark, cold houses. . . . We can put sea walls around New York and New Jersey [to deal with rising ocean levels]. . . . I'm not saying it's going to be pretty but we can live with it."[46] But for those investing in clean tech and green tech, such attitudes are seriously out of date. They see a world changing fast, and they plan to make money and help cool the planet at the same time.

"Our generation has inherited an incredibly beautiful world from our parents and they from their parents. We must not be the generation responsible for irreversibly damaging the environment."[43]

—Richard Branson, CEO of Virgin Atlantic Airlines.

FACTS

- Because of its reliance on cars, buses, air-conditioning, and air travel, the tourism industry is responsible for 5 percent of the world's carbon dioxide emissions.

- The Phoenix Motorcars company is building a sports utility truck (SUT) powered by a unique battery that allows the vehicle to travel 100 miles (161km) on a 10-minute charge from a special high-voltage charger.

- In January 2007 Continental Airlines successfully flew a Boeing 737 jet with fuel made from 50 percent algae oil and jatropha, a weed that bears oil-producing seeds.

- In 2008 Google customized a fleet of plug-in hybrid vehicles for its employees to test drive. The Toyota Prius with a plug-in conversion module averaged over 93 miles per gallon (39.5 km per L) in mixed city and highway driving.

- In 2008, as part of its "Greening State Capitols" partnership, Wal-Mart sent energy audit teams to over 20 state capitols to find ways for state-owned buildings to reduce energy consumption and lower CO_2 emissions.

What Lifestyle Changes Are Needed?

I n 2007 Rupert Murdoch, president of the huge media conglom-
erate News Corporation, decided he wanted to make his company carbon neutral by 2010. News Corporation (News Corp)
owns dozens of major businesses including the *Wall Street Journal*,
Fox News, 20th Century Fox film productions, and MySpace. Together, Murdoch's companies generate $28 billion a year in revenue,
employ 64,000 people, and contribute 706,000 tons (640,000t) of
CO_2 annually to the atmosphere.

Murdoch, who is known for his ultraconservative, pro-business
views, shocked many when he began his campaign to lower News
Corp's carbon footprint. When announcing his plan to reduce
emissions, Murdoch said he will use his media empire to educate
the public about climate change issues because global warming will
get worse until individuals change their habits:

> The climate problem will not be solved without mass par-
> ticipation by the general public in countries around the
> globe. And that's where we come in. Our audience's car-
> bon footprint is 10,000 times bigger than ours. That's the
> carbon footprint we want to conquer. We cannot do it
> with gimmicks. We need to reach them in a sustained way.
> To weave this issue into our content—make it dramatic,
> make it vivid, even sometimes make it fun. We want to
> inspire people to change their behavior.[47]

Many scientists agree with Murdoch. While it is easy to blame big businesses for global warming, individuals also have a role to play in reducing greenhouse gases. Global warming could be greatly reduced if each person drove fewer miles, used less electricity, and even changed their eating habits a little bit. While making personal sacrifices is harder than blaming corporations and the government, Chris Goodall writes in *How to Live a Low-Carbon Lifestyle*: "We cannot hide behind an unjustified expectation that political or corporate leaders are going to do something for us: the threat of climate change requires each of us to take personal responsibility for reducing our impact on the planet's atmosphere."[48]

Rupert Murdoch, whose News Corporation owns dozens of major media businesses, announced in 2007 that his company would strive to dramatically cut its carbon output and educate the public about climate change.

Changing personal behavior has many positive benefits. For example, riding a bicycle to school or work instead of driving does more than reduce global warming gases. One hour of moderate pedaling can burn 500 calories. Since more than half of all Americans are overweight, bicycle commuting can help reduce the obesity and diabetes epidemics in the United States while slowing climate change.

Global Warming and Food

The health of the atmosphere is also affected by the quantity and type of food people eat. Food production is the most carbon-intensive activity in the world. Massive amounts of fossil fuels are used to plant and harvest crops. Oil, natural gas, and coal are used to manufacture fertilizers and pesticides and apply them to fields. Oil is used to power the trucks, trains, ships, and airplanes that transport food. When turned into products for consumers, food processors, distributors, and supermarkets all consume huge amounts of electricity for lighting, refrigeration, and other functions. When the food is finally on the grocers' shelves, consumers drive to the market, spewing about 1 pound (0.45 kg) of CO_2 for every mile (1.6 km) driven. When taken together, food production adds over 2 tons (1.8 t) of greenhouse gas emissions to each individual American's total every year. This is about one-fifth of the annual global warming gases produced by each person.

While most consumer food production contributes to global warming, cattle ranching has the largest impact. According to a 2006 report from the United Nations Food and Agriculture Organization, beef production generates more greenhouse gas emissions than the transportation sector. This pollution is produced by cows, animals that belch and pass gas constantly. The methane gas they produce with this flatulence has a heat-trapping power 23 times more powerful than CO_2. While people tend to laugh when discussing cow flatulence and global warming, scientists say it is a serious problem since there are more than 1.3 billion cows on Earth, with 100 million in the United States. In 2007, a United Nations report stated that the world's cattle account for 18 percent of all greenhouse gas emissions.

Each cow expels 158 gallons (598 L) of methane a day, which translates to 11.6 pounds (5.3 kg) of methane created for every pound (0.45 kg) of beef that it produces. This is nearly triple the amount of CO_2 created through pork and chicken production. Cow manure also emits methane, especially when stored in sewage lagoons on large-scale, industrial cattle farms. In addition, manure

> "The climate problem will not be solved without mass participation by the general public in countries around the globe."[47]
>
> —Rupert Murdoch, CEO of News Corporation.

Reducing Your Own Carbon Footprint

Laura Stec and Eugene Cordero, authors of the book *Cool Cuisine*, provide a list of questions consumers can ask themselves to determine the carbon footprint created by the meals they eat. The authors believe that individuals can reduce their carbon footprint by changing their eating habits. They suggest changes such as using fewer animal products, fewer processed foods, less bottled water, and more fresh, organic, seasonal, and locally grown whole foods. The questions appear below.

- How far do I travel to buy food and how do I get there?
- How much food am I buying—will I eat it all?
- What kind of food am I buying—is it plant based or animal based?
- Geographically, where is my food coming from?
- Is my food organic?
- How processed is my food?
- What kind of packaging is used for my food?
- Do I buy too many processed foods that need to be frozen or refrigerated?
- How am I disposing of the food and packaging waste?

Laura Stec and Eugene Cordero, *How About a Cool Cuisine?* The Global Warming Diet, 2009. www.globalwarmingdiet.org.

lagoons emit nitrous oxide, a gas with 300 times the global warming potential of CO_2.

While cows add to global warming problems, world demand for beef is increasing every year. For example, in 2008 people in China ate twice as much beef as they did in 1998. However, the Chinese eat only 10 pounds (4.5 kg) of beef per capita annually, while the average American eats 67 pounds (30.4 kg).

Scientist Jim Hansen recommends individuals reduce their beef consumption to lower their carbon footprint. Experts say that if every American ate one less serving of beef a week, it would be equal to taking 5 million cars off the road. As Israeli food researcher Gidon Eshel states, a person "doesn't have to be all the way to the extreme end of [becoming a] vegan. If you simply cut down from two burgers a week to one, you've already made a substantial difference."[49] By doing this every person could save 3,300 pounds (1,500 kg) of emissions a year.

Cars and Carbon Dioxide

When most people sit down for a meal, they do not equate global warming gases with the food on their plate. The emissions are created far from the kitchen in rural farm fields, isolated slaughterhouses, centralized food warehouses, and on open highways. But other individual behavior, such as driving, has a much more obvious impact on global warming.

Cows produce huge amounts of methane gas, which makes cattle ranching and beef production one of the biggest generators of greenhouse gases. Some ranchers are trying ways of capturing the methane gas for use as a power source.

People can directly affect how much CO_2 they produce by carpooling. If one person drives 20 miles (32 km) to work in an average American car, he or she is pumping 20 pounds (9 kg) of CO_2 into the atmosphere. If three people carpool with that driver, each one is only producing 5 pounds (2.2 kg) of CO_2 to get to work.

Motorists can also reduce their emissions by driving conservatively. Fast acceleration and hard breaking reduces gas mileage by as much as 33 percent. This means when a driver races from red light to red light in a typical SUV like a Ford Expedition, he or she is getting 8 miles per gallon (3.4 km per L) instead of 12 miles per gallon (5.1 km per L). This type of driving is wasteful and also pointless since it does not save time. One study found that quick starts and hard stops reduce travel time by only about 4 percent or 75 seconds on a 30-minute trip.

In addition to easing off on the throttle, drivers also improve fuel economy with simple maintenance. For example, tires that are underinflated reduce gas mileage by 3.5 percent. While this number may seem small, about one quarter of all cars, SUVs, and pickup trucks on the road in the United States have at least one tire that is low on air. According to the Department of Energy, that means about 1.2 billion gallons (4.5 billion L) of gas were wasted in 2005 as a result of underinflated tires. And that gasoline produced 24 billion pounds (10.9 billion kg) of CO_2.

Another way individuals can have an impact on global warming is by purchasing energy efficient cars. A motorist who drives 12,000 miles (19,300 km) a year in a Toyota Prius hybrid contributes 5,160 pounds (2,340 kg) of carbon dioxide to the atmosphere annually. That same driver in a Toyota Tacoma pickup truck adds about twice as much pollution, 11,260 pounds (5,107 kg). And an individual in a Cadillac Escalade SUV pumps 16,680 pounds (7,566 kg) of CO_2 into the air, more than three times the global warming gas produced by the Prius.

Hypermilers

Some people are not content to achieve 20 or even 40 miles per gallon (8 km or 16 km per L). A Chicago man named Wayne Gerdes has devised driving techniques that help him attain over 100 miles per gallon (42 km per L) in a Honda Civic Hybrid, which normally gets about 45 miles per gallon (19 km per L). He also achieves 59 miles per gallon (25 km per L) from a standard Honda Accord, a car rated by the EPA to achieve 31 miles per gallon (13 km per L) in normal driving conditions.

Gerdes invented the term hypermiler for a new breed of driver who is pushing the limits of fuel efficiency to record levels. Since heavier cars consume more gas, Gerdes removes nearly everything from his car that is not attached to the body, including the jack and spare tire and items in the glove compartment. He even leaves his shoes and wallet behind when he competes for the title of Most Fuel-Efficient Driver in the World in a 20-mile race (32 km), the Hybridfest MPG Challenge, held on the streets of Madison, Wisconsin.

Even in everyday driving Gerdes gets high gas mileage by accelerating at incredibly slow speeds, creeping forward while barely raising the engine past idle speed. When it comes time to make a turn, he lets off the gas pedal well ahead of the intersection so his car slows naturally. This way he does not have to step on the brakes. On interstate highways, Gerdes drives just a steady 49 miles (79 km) per hour, the most efficient speed for gas economy.

Even on the hottest days, Gerdes never uses a car's energy-consuming air conditioner and always drives with the windows rolled up to increase efficiency. In parking lots, the hypermiler parks his car facing outward on the isolated edges of the lot, which are often angled slightly downward. From these areas he can start by rolling forward without using his engine. Using this technique, called the face-out, Gerdes does not have to waste gas by backing up, applying his brakes, and moving forward like a normal driver.

Gerdes says he began hypermiling to help reduce America's dependence on foreign oil and to help slow global warming, "I'm not just doing this for myself. I'm doing this for my country and the world."[50] And Gerdes is not alone. When gas prices spiked to over $3 a gallon in 2006, thousands of drivers began hypermiling, posting their mileage figures on Internet Web sites such as www.cleanmpg.com, which boasted in December 2008 that its members collectively saved 263,669 gallons (998,000 L) of

"The threat of climate change requires each of us to take personal responsibility for reducing our impact on the planet's atmosphere."[48]

—Chris Goodall, author of *How to Live a Low-Carbon Lifestyle* and *Ten Technologies to Save the Planet.*

The Problem with Carbon Offsets

Environmentalist George Monbiot is a critic of carbon offsets. He believes they do little to reduce carbon dioxide emissions in the developed world, as he explains on his Web site:

> The problem is this. If runaway climate change is not to trigger the irreversible melting of the Greenland and West Antarctic ice sheets and drive hundreds of millions of people from their homes . . . [it will require] a 60% cut in global climate emissions by 2030, which means a 90% cut in the rich world. Even if, through carbon offset schemes carried out in developing countries, every poor nation on the planet became carbon-free, we would still have to cut most of the carbon we produce at home. . . . By selling us a clean conscience, the offset companies are undermining the necessary political battle to tackle climate change at home. They are telling us that we don't need to be citizens; we need only be better consumers.

George Monbiot, "Selling Indulgences," Monibot.com, October 19, 2006. www.monbiot.com.

fuel. Of course, the hypermilers would save more gas by riding on public transportation. A commuter taking a city bus 8,000 (12,875 km) miles to work every year contributes only 311 pounds (141kg) of CO_2 to the atmosphere, 26 times less than the driver in a Prius.

Bright Light Ideas

After transportation, the second biggest source of CO_2 generation comes from power plants. Those who wish to help stop climate change can make a difference by regulating their use of heating, cooling, lighting, and other power consumption.

In recent years millions of individuals have lowered their carbon footprint and their electric bills by switching to compact fluorescent lamps (CFLs). These bulbs, which fit into almost any light socket, produce the same amount of light as standard incandescent bulbs while using less than one-third of the power.

The savings of CFLs are obvious since an average home has 40 lightbulbs. The cost of lighting adds about $200 to a household's annual electricity bill. Compact fluorescents can reduce that bill by $66 a year. While CFLs cost more than standard bulbs, the one-year savings pays to replace nearly all the old-fashioned incandescent bulbs. And the CFLs will not burn out for seven years, so the savings multiply year after year.

In addition to reducing costs, CFLs provide a quick, easy way to slow global warming. According to the government's Energy Star Web site, if everyone in the United States changed just a single 60-watt bulb in their home to a CFL, "we would save enough energy to light more than 2.5 million homes for a year and prevent greenhouse gases equivalent to the emissions of nearly 800,000 cars."[51] And if only one lightbulb were changed per house, it would save $3 billion in electrical costs and prevent 20 million tons (18 million t) of greenhouse gases from spewing out of power plants.

The savings from CFLs are so great that the European Union banned the sale of incandescent lights starting in 2010 as part of an aggressive energy policy to fight climate change. California, Australia, and Canada are considering similar bans. The bulbs are not perfect, however. They contain 4 milligrams of mercury, a dangerous poison, so discarded bulbs need to be recycled. And if someone breaks a CFL, the EPA recommends that the room be vacated for 15 minutes with a window left open so the air can clear of mercury contamination.

Power from the Sun

With millions of people switching to CFLs, the cost of the bulbs has dropped dramatically. In 1999 the bulbs cost up to $8 each, but as demand grew, more manufacturers began producing the bulbs and competing for customers. In 2009 CFLs were selling for under $3 a piece and were occasionally on sale at large discount stores for about a dollar.

Supporters of solar power are hoping that a similar price plunge will be seen in the cost of solar panels (also called photovoltaic or PV cells). The sun provides more energy to Earth every day than could be consumed by the entire population of Earth in 27 years. If that energy was harnessed for electricity, global warming emissions would be drastically reduced. However, in 2008 solar power cost about 6 times more than electricity from coal-fired power plants. Therefore, a homeowner would have to spend about $20,000 on solar panels to lower his electric bill by $150 a month. But while it would take more than 11 years for the panels to pay for themselves, the homeowner would generate about 151,630 pounds (68,765kg) less CO_2 during that period.

Bright news is on the horizon for solar power. Experts are predicting that by 2012, the cost of solar will be cheaper than coal due to the discovery of an advanced PV cell manufacturing technique using nanotechnology. The new production method can be used to create solar cells that are 100,000 times smaller than the width of a human hair.

Experimental nano–solar cells are being printed onto thin rolls of flexible plastic film. Sheets of the film collect more light than traditional PV cells of the same size. Manufacturing costs are about one-tenth of traditional silicon cells, and the sheets of film can be rolled across any rooftop or built into roofing materials. The first application of the film will likely be in cell phones and other electronic devices, replacing rechargeable batteries like those used today. However, some believe that the nanosolar-cell film could replace all fossil fuel power plants in the United States within 30 years.

Buying Carbon Offsets

One path people have been following to slow global warming has nothing to do with high-tech solar cells or expensive hybrid cars. In recent years individuals have been able to balance the CO_2 they produce by making payments to companies that plant trees, build wind farms, or invest other renewable energy projects. The voluntary payments are called carbon offsets.

"I'm not just doing this for myself. I'm doing this for my country and the world." [50]

—Wayne Gerdes, inventor of hypermiler driving techniques.

Carbon offsets have become big business on the Internet since 2003. Companies such as TerraPass and CarbonFund.org provide carbon calculators that allow individuals to estimate their carbon footprint by determining how far they travel, what type of car they have, and how much electricity they use. The calculator provides a figure in tons of CO_2 produced. People can then pay about $10 a ton for carbon offsets. For example, the average American produces over 19 tons (17.2 t) of CO_2 annually. Someone wishing to offset their 19 tons pays $190 to one of dozens of companies that invest in mitigation projects.

Carbon offsets go to hundreds of different types of projects. For example, the Climate Trust invests in regional projects such as preserving a native forest in Oregon and upgrading a paper manufacturer in Portland to be more energy efficient. TerraPass invests in biomass energy projects such as trapping methane produced by cows on dairy farms and using the gas as a fuel source. Carbonfund.org uses offsets to build renewable-energy systems for low-income families.

Compact fluorescent lightbulbs allow consumers to reduce their carbon footprint and save money on electric bills. These bulbs produce the same amount of light as standard incandescent bulbs but use less than one-third of the power.

Carbon offsets—or the paying of companies that plant trees, build wind farms, or invest in other renewable energy projects—are being used more as a way for people and companies to offset their carbon footprint. One company invested in preserving the native forests in Oregon and making a paper manufacturer more efficient.

Like many other methods meant to reduce global warming gases, carbon offsets have generated controversy. The market is unregulated, and anyone can set up a Web site to collect money from people who feel guilty about their energy-consuming lifestyles. While Climate Trust spends 92 percent of the money it collects on offsets, TerraPass does not divulge how much money it keeps and what percentage goes to Earth-friendly projects. However, research conducted by *Business Week* estimated TerraPass spent about 25 percent of the money. Whatever the case, many companies are seeing the profit potential in carbon reduction, and the number of companies offering offsets is growing. For example, when people buy airline tickets through Expedia, they can also purchase carbon offsets to mitigate the CO_2 produced by the flight.

As a growing number of individuals are made aware of their carbon footprint, carbon offset schemes will continue to proliferate. And as each person takes steps to drive less, convert to solar, or buy offsets, the climate of Earth will slowly improve. Optimists believe that within a hundred years, homes and cars will be powered by renewables, methane will be recycled, and solar panels and wind turbines will generate most electricity. If this proves to be true, experts believe global warming can be slowed and eventually reversed.

FACTS

- By reducing the temperature on a home's thermostat by 2°F (1°C) in the winter, a homeowner can save $100 a year while cutting CO_2 emissions.

- Household lighting in the United States is responsible for up to 160 million tons (145 million t) of CO_2 emissions per year.

- If the majority of U.S. PC computer owners used the energy-saving features in Windows Vista, they would prevent 3 million tons (2.7 million t) of global warming pollution from being emitted from electric power plants.

- Hypermiler Wayne Gerdes drove his hybrid Toyota Prius 800 miles (1,287 km) from Chicago to New York City on 8.9 gallons (33.7 L) of gas, for an average of 71 miles per gallon (38 km per L). His tank held 12 gallons (45.4 L), leaving him a quarter of a tank at the end of the trip.

- Travelers wishing to charge their iPods, cell phones, and notebook computers with renewable energy can purchase backpacks outfitted with mini–solar panels for about $200.

Related Organizations

Carbon Trade Watch

PO Box 14656
1001 LD Amsterdam
The Netherlands
phone: 31 20 662 66 08
fax: 31 20 675 71 76
e-mail: info@carbontradewatch.org
Web site: www.carbontradewatch.org

Carbon Trade Watch is a European organization established to provide citizen oversight of carbon trading schemes. Members feel cap-and-trade systems are being manipulated by major corporations to allow them to pollute more, not less. A fundamental aspect of their work is producing in-depth research on pollution trading, which members believe is severely lacking. Carbon Trade Watch publishes about a dozen books and allows free downloads of various publications such as *The Sky Is Not the Limit* from its Web site. The group also provides related videos, audio links, and photo essays.

Center for the Study of Carbon Dioxide and Global Change

PO Box 25697
Tempe, AZ 85285-5697
phone: (480) 966-3719
Web site: http://co2science.org

This organization was founded by scientists who believe that man-made CO_2 is increasing in the atmosphere, but this phenomenon is not the cause of rising global temperatures. The organization publishes an online weekly publication *CO₂ Science* magazine.

The Climate Trust

65 SW Yamhill St., Suite 400
Portland, OR 97204
phone: (503) 238-1915
e-mail: info@climatetrust.org
Web site: www.climatetrust.org

The Climate Trust funds projects that remove carbon dioxide from the atmosphere. These include investing in renewable energy, planting forests, and giving grants to those interested in increasing energy efficiency in buildings, factories, or transportation. The group's partner Web site Carboncounter.org allows users to estimate how much annual carbon dioxide is produced by their day-to-day activities.

Competitive Enterprise Institute (CEI)

1001 Connecticut Ave. NW, Suite 1250
Washington, DC 20036
phone: (202) 331-1010
fax: (202) 331-0640
e-mail: info@cei.org
Web site: www.cei.org

CEI encourages the use of the free market and private property rights to protect the environment. It advocates removing governmental regulatory barriers and establishing a system in which the private sector would be responsible for the environment. CEI publications include research papers, news releases, a monthly newsletter, blogs, and op-ed articles.

Energy Information Administration (EIA)

1000 Independence Ave. SW
Washington, DC 20585
phone: (202) 586-8800
e-mail: InfoCtr@eia.doe.gov
Web site: www.eia.doe.gov

The Energy Information Administration (EIA) is an agency of the U.S. Department of Energy that provides data, forecasts, and analyses regarding energy and its interaction with the economy and the environment. The EIA's "Energy Kid's Page" provides energy facts, games, classroom activities, and energy history lessons. The agency publishes dozens of reports including *Annual Energy Outlook, Renewable Energy Trends*, and *Greenhouse Gases, Climate Change, and Energy*.

Greenpeace USA

75 Arkansas St., Suite 1
San Francisco, CA 94197
phone: (415) 255-9221
e-mail: info@wdc.greenpeace.org
Web site: www.greenpeace.org

Greenpeace is an activist environmental organization whose members use peaceful direct action to stop global warming, the destruction of ancient forests, whaling, and nuclear proliferation. The group publishes online blogs, press releases, and detailed reports on global warming and other issues.

The Heritage Foundation

214 Massachusetts Ave. NE
Washington, DC 20002
phone: (800) 544-4843
fax: (202) 544-2260
e-mail: pubs@heritage.org
Web site: www.heritage.org

The Heritage Foundation is a conservative think tank that supports the principles of free enterprise and limited government on global warming matters. Its many publications include the following position papers: "Can No One Stop the EPA?" and "How to Help the Environment Without Destroying Jobs."

The National Renewable Energy Laboratory (NREL)

1617 Cole Blvd.
Golden, CO 80401-3393
phone: (303) 275-3000
Web site: www.nrel.gov

The National Renewable Energy Laboratory (NREL) is the U.S. Department of Energy's laboratory for renewable energy research, development, and deployment, and a leading laboratory for energy efficiency. Some of the areas of scientific investigation at NREL include wind energy, biomass-derived fuels, advanced vehicles, solar manufacturing, hydrogen fuel cells, and waste-to-energy technologies. The organization publishes dozens of comprehensive research papers concerning these technologies, many of them available for free online.

Natural Resources Defense Council (NRDC)
40 West 20th St.
New York, NY 10011
phone: (212) 727-2700
fax: (212) 727-1773
e-mail: nrdcinfo@nrdc.org
Web site: www.nrdc.org

The Natural Resources Defense Council (NRDC) uses law, science, and the support of 1.2 million members and online activists to protect the environment. Its global warming Web page (www.nrdc.org/globalwarming) contains details on global warming legislation and provides ways for consumers to shrink their carbon footprint. The NRDC publishes *On Earth*, a quarterly magazine; *Nature's Voice*, a bimonthly online magazine; and various reports and e-mail bulletins.

Sierra Club
85 2nd St., 2nd Floor
San Francisco, CA 94105-3441
phone: (415) 977-5500
fax: (415) 977-5799
e-mail: information@sierraclub.org
Web site: www.sierraclub.org

The Sierra Club is a nonprofit public interest organization that promotes conservation of the natural environment by influencing public policy decisions. The group provides extensive coverage of issues such as renewable energy, clean cars, and energy efficiency. The club publishes *Sierra* magazine, the *Sierra Club Insider* e-newsletter, several blogs, and dozens of books on the environment.

Union of Concerned Scientists (UCS)

2 Brattle Square
Cambridge, MA 02238-9105
phone: (617) 547-5552
fax: (617) 864-9405
e-mail: www.ucsusa.org
Web site: www.ucsusa.org

The Union of Concerned Scientists is a science-based organization that combines independent scientific research and citizen action to develop practical solutions to environmental problems and to secure responsible changes in government policy, corporate practices, and consumer choices. The group provides reports on global warming, clean energy, clean vehicles, and other environmental issues. In addition, UCS publishes Catalyst magazine, *Earthwise* newsletter, and *Greentips*, an e-newsletter with environmental information for consumers.

For Further Research

Books

Agnieszka Biskup, *Understanding Global Warming with Max Axiom, Super Scientist*. Mankato, MN: Capstone, 2008.

Paul Brown, *Global Warning*. Pleasantville, NY: Reader's Digest, 2007.

Iain Carson and Vijay V. Vaitheeswaran, *Zoom: The Global Race to Fuel the Car of the Future*. New York: Twelve, 2008.

Lynne Cherry, *How We Know What We Know About Our Changing Climate: Scientists and Kids Explore Global Warming*. Nevada City, CA: Dawn, 2008.

Laurie David, *The Down-to-Earth Guide to Global Warming*. New York: Orchard Books, 2007.

Kirstin Dow, *The Atlas of Climate Change: Mapping the World's Greatest Challenge*. Berkeley: University of California Press, 2007.

Jeri Freedman, *Climate Change: Human Effects on the Nitrogen Cycle*. New York: Rosen, 2007.

Christopher C. Horner, *The Politically Incorrect Guide to Global Warming and Environmentalism*. Washington, DC: Regnery, 2007.

Jane O'Connor, *An Inconvenient Truth: The Crisis of Global Warming*. New York: Viking, 2007.

Matthew Robinson, *America Debates Global Warming: Crisis or Myth?* New York: Rosen Central, 2008.

Web Sites

Al Gore (www.algore.com). A Web site maintained by the former vice president, a leading activist in the environmental movement. The site contains blogs, speeches, and links to organizations dedicated to fighting global warming.

Aptera (www.aptera.com). The Web site for the three-wheel, aerodynamic, lightweight car called Aptera, made from recycled materials and meant to go 300 miles on a gallon of gas or 100 miles on an electrical charge.

Climate Crisis Jam (www.climatecrisisjam.org). This Web site features original music videos by Earthman and others who rap and sing about global warming and the environment.

Earth Observatory (http://earthobservatory.nasa.gov/Features/GlobalWarming). A site maintained by NASA with images of Earth from space; articles about global warming solutions; and global maps showing scientific data such as wildfire locations, rainfall, and land surface temperatures.

Global Warming: Early Warning Signs (www.climatehotmap.org/about.html). An interactive map that illustrates the local consequences of global warming throughout the world. The Fingerprints category shows locations where storms, environmental damage, and other consequences of global warming have occurred. The Harbingers category identifies places where recent trends, such as disappearing species, are early warning signs of global warming problems to come.

Global Warming Interactive (http://environment.nationalgeographic.com/environment/global-warming/gw-overview.html). This site, published by *National Geographic,* features articles, videos, music, art, and photography concerning global warming. Information is provided about biofuels, deforestation, fuel cells, and dozens of other related topics.

"Hot Politics" (www.pbs.org/wgbh/pages/frontline/hotpolitics). A PBS *Frontline* investigation into the politics behind global warming in the United States. The page features a streaming video of the TV program, reports on suppressed science, views of global warming skeptics, and alternative energy solutions.

Junkscience.com (http://junkscience.com). A Web site dedicated to debunking what its author, Steven J. Milloy, alleges to be false claims regarding global warming, DDT, cigarette smoking, and other topics. Milloy is a frequent guest on *FOX News* and a paid spokesman for Phillip Morris, ExxonMobil, and other corporations.

Pew Center on Global Climate Change (www.pewclimate.org). The Pew Center on Global Climate Change is a nonprofit, nonpartisan organization dedicated to providing credible information and innovative solutions in the effort to address global climate change. Its Web site features the latest global warming news and provides dozens of publications from international, federal, state, and business sources.

World View of Global Warming (www.worldviewofglobalwarming.org). Photographic documentation of global warming with pictures of Antarctica, the Arctic, glaciers, temperate zone, oceans, and weather events. Photos are accompanied by explanations of how each topic is related to global warming.

Source Notes

Introduction: A Scientific and Political Problem

1. Quoted in Patrick O'Driscoll, "El Nino Gives USA Its Hottest Year in '06," *USA Today*, January 10, 2007. www.usatoday.com.

Chapter One: What Are the Origins of the Global Warming Issue?

2. Quoted in William K. Stevens, "If Climate Changes, It May Change Quickly," *New York Times*, January 27, 1998. http://query.nytimes.com.

3. Quoted in Helen Briggs, "50 Years On: The Keeling Curve Legacy," BBC News, December 2, 2007. http://news.bbc.co.uk.

4. Al Gore, *An Inconvenient Truth*. Emmaus, PA: Rodale, 2006, p. 40.

5. Quoted in Spencer Wert, "The Discovery of Global Warming," American Institute of Physics, 2008. www.aip.org.

6. Quoted in Meteor Blades, "Blast from the Past—James Hansen, 1988," *Daily Kos*, January 14, 2008. www.dailykos.com.

7. Quoted in William K. Stevens, *The Change in the Weather: People, Weather and the Science of Climate*. New York: Delacorte, 1999, p. 133.

8. Thomas Friedman, *Hot, Flat, and Crowded*. New York: Farrar, Straus and Giroux, 2008, p. 15.

9. Quoted in Spencer Wert, "Government: The View from Washington, DC," American Institute of Physics, 2008. www.aip.org.

10. Quoted in Greenpeace, "ExxonSecrets Fact Sheet," May 2007. www.exxonsecrets.org.

11. Quoted in Philip Shabecoff, "E.P.A. Report Says Earth Will Heat Up Beginning in 1990's," *New York Times*, October 18, 1983, p. 1.

12. Intergovernmental Panel on Climate Change, "Executive Summary," Columbia University, 2008. www.ciesin.org.

13. Wert, "Government: The View from Washington, DC."

14. Nobelprize.org, "The Nobel Peace Prize 2007," 2008. http://nobelprize.org.

15. Quoted in Friedman, *Hot, Flat, and Crowded*, p. 43.

Chapter Two: How Should Developing Nations Respond?

16. Quoted in Friedman, *Hot, Flat, and Crowded*, p. 55.

17. Quoted in Associated Press, "Global Warming Will Strike Developing Nations the Hardest, UN Says," *International Herald Tribune*, August 7, 2007. www.iht.com.

18. Quoted in WISTA, "In Focus," Waterfalls Institute of Technology Transfer," October 2008. www.witts.org.

19. Salil Tripathi, "Escaping the 'Hindu Rate of Growth,'" *Guardian Unlimited*, June 13, 2006. www.guardian.co.uk.

20. Quoted in Friedman, *Hot, Flat, and Crowded*, p. 345.

21. Quoted in Friedman, *Hot, Flat, and Crowded*, p. 345.

22. Quoted in Embassy of the People's Republic of China, "China Issues National Plan to Address Climate Change," June 5, 2007. www.fmprc.gov.cn.

23. Quoted in Embassy of the People's Republic of China, "China Issues National Plan to Address Climate Change."

Chapter Three: How Should Developed Nations Respond?

24. Bruce Alberts et al., *Lighting the Way*, InterAcademy Council, 2007. www.interacademycouncil.net.

25. Quoted in Weathervane, "United Kingdom's Fuel Economy Label," Resources for the Future, 2008. www.weathervane.rff.org.

26. Kevin Smith, "Obscenity of Carbon Trading," Carbon Trade Watch, November 6, 2006. www.carbontradewatch.org.

27. Quoted in Karsten Stumm, "Killing Jobs to Save the Climate?" *Business Week*, July 18, 2008. www.businessweek.com.

28. Quoted in Ross Gelbspan, *Boiling Point*. New York: Basic Books, 2004, p. 37.

29. Quoted in Gelbspan, *Boiling Point*, p. 41.

30. Quoted in Associated Press, "Science Posts Go to Activists on Warming," *Los Angeles Times*, December 21, 2008, p. A24.

31. Quoted in Tim Dickinson, "The Secret Campaign of President Bush's Administration to Deny Global Warming," *Rolling Stone*, June 28, 2007. www.rollingstone.com.

32. Quoted in Katie Fehrenbacher, "Former Energy Secretaries: Cap and Trade Is Bad for Business," *Earth2Tech*, November 12, 2008. http://earth2tech.com.

33. Quoted in Associated Press, "Science Posts Go to Activists on Warming," p. A24.

34. Quoted in Edward Helmore, "Obama's Revolution on Climate Change," *Guardian UK*, December 21, 2008. www.guardian.co.uk.

Chapter Four: How Should Business and Industry Respond?

35. A. Hoffman, "Getting Ahead of the Curve: Corporate Strategies That Address Climate Change," Pew Center on Global Climate Change, 2006. www.pewclimate.org.

36. Pew Center on Global Climate Change, "Climate Change 101: Business Strategies," 2008. www.pewclimate.org.

37. Quoted in CBS News, "Could the Electric Car Save Us?" September 16, 2007. www.cbsnews.com.

38. GM Media Online, "Chevrolet Volt Media Site," 2008. http://media.gm.com.

39. Brian Dumaine, *The Plot to Save the Planet*. New York: Crown Business, 2008, p. 21.

40. Quoted in Steven Mufson, "Blueprint for 'Car 2.0,'" *Los Angeles Times*, December 27, 2008, p. C2.

41. Quoted in Mufson, "Blueprint for 'Car 2.0,'" p. C2.

42. Quoted in Mufson, "Blueprint for 'Car 2.0,'" p. C2.

43. Quoted in MSNBC, "Branson Bets Billions to Curb Global Warming," September 26, 2006. www.msnbc.msn.com.

44. Quoted in Stephen Leahy, "Environment: Biofuels Boom Spurring Deforestation," InterPress Service, March 21, 2007. http://ipsnews.net.

45. Quoted in Chuck Squatriglia, "Virgin Atlantic Biofuel Flight—Green Breakthrough or Greenwash?" *Wired Blog* Network, February 25, 2008. http://blog.wired.com.

46. Dumaine, *The Plot to Save the Planet*, p. 14.

Chapter Five: What Lifestyle Changes Are Needed?

47. Quoted in Mark Lynas, "Can Murdoch Save the Planet?" Guardian, May 17, 2007. www.guardian.co.uk.

48. Chris Goodall, *How to Live a Low-Carbon Lifestyle*. London: Earthscan, 2007, p. 3.

49. Quoted in Brad Knickerbocker, "Humans' Beef with Livestock: A Warmer Planet," *Christian Science Monitor*, February 20, 2007. www.csmonitor.com.

50. Quoted in Dennis Gaffney, "This Guy Can Get 59 MPG in a Plain Old Accord. Beat That, Punk," *Mother Jones*, January/February 2007. www.motherjones.com.

51. Energy Star, "Use Compact Florescent Lighting," 2008. www.energystar.gov.

Index

About the Author

Stuart A. Kallen has written more than 250 nonfiction books for children and young adults over the past 20 years. His books have covered countless aspects of human history, culture, and science from the building of the pyramids to the music of the twenty-first century. Some of his recent titles include *How Should the World Respond to Global Warming?, Romantic Art*, and *The World Energy Crisis*. Kallen, who lives in San Diego, California, is also a singer-songwriter and guitarist.